CHINESE LANDSCAPE
G A R D E N I N G

CHINESE LANDSCAPE

FOREIGN LANGUAGES PRESS BEIJING CHINA

Compiled by Zhu Junzhen
Managing Editor Xiao Shiling
Translated by Yan Jie
English Editor Peng Ruifu
Designed by Wang Zhi
Photographs by Zhu Junzhen and others

First Edition   1992

ISBN 0-8351-2416-9
ISBN 7-119-01252-5
Copyright 1992 by Foreign Languages Press, Beijing, China
Published by Foreign Languages Press
24 Baiwanzhuang Road, Beijing 100037, China

Printed in the People's Republic of China

Contents

Chapter Three

Chapter Four

Chapter Five

Chapter Six

PAGE 129

PAGE 144

PAGE 156

Preface

I. History of Chinese Gardens

Starting with the *you* (park) in the 16th century B.C., gardening art in China traces its history back to more than 3,000 years. It developed in two embryonic forms during the long years of feudal society.

The first form had its source in the *chunpu you* (pure and simple park) of the Yin and Zhou dynasties (1766-770 B.C.). Emperors used these natural parks to raise birds and animals for entertainment and hunting. Historical records show that Emperor Wen Wang (11th century B.C.) of the Zhou Dynasty had a huge *you* where common people could go to cut grass or raise pheasants and rabbits. In the Qin and Han dynasties (221 B.C.-A.D. 220), emperors were no longer satisfied with natural parks and had groups of buildings erected in the areas around the imperial court to attest to their dignity. This kind of garden was called "palace gardens." The Efang Palace of the Qin Dynasty (221-206 B.C.) is an example where halls and pavilions were built in close order (Figure 0-1). Another example was the Shanglin Garden of the Han Dynasty (206 B.C.-A.D. 220), where 70 palaces were built in an area extending 150 kilometres. Various kinds of animals were raised there, including 1,000 horses.

After the Sui and Tang dynasties (589-907), Chinese garden designers began to pay more attention to the utilization of natural scenery with hills, lakes, and streams, and so another kind of garden was created: "imperial garden with hills and water." Notable among gardens of this period was the Xiyuan Garden of Sui Dynasty (589-618) with 16 courtyards containing fish ponds and vegetable gardens. The borders of the entire area were about 50 kilometres long. The Genyu Garden of the Song Dynasty (960-1280) gave more emphasis to the shapes of hills, water courses and rocks. This style lasted to the Ming and Qing dynasties (1368-1911) and traces of it can still be seen in the Summer Palace in Beijing and the imperial summer resort in Chengde (Figures 0-2 and 0-3). Technical design and the art of landscaping with hills, water, and rocks reached a high level in these gardens. They are therefore considered excellent examples of one form of traditional Chinese garden.

Another form was born during the Spring and Autumn Period (770-221 B.C.), when the natural beauty of mountains and water was preferred. This form was greatly influenced by Chinese literature and painting in the process of its development. According to ancient records, Jingu (Golden Valley) Garden of the Western Jin period (265-316) had beautiful landscapes with clear water, a fish pond, and luxuriant foliage, including fruit trees, bamboo, pine, and medicinal herbs. The Hualin Garden of the Eastern Jin period (317-420) featured towering trees, hanging wisteria vines and narrow, rocky paths winding over gullies. These two parks were representative of the natural gardens of that time.

The Tang and Song dynasties were a golden period of literature and art. Influenced by the literary flair of great contemporary writers and poets, the garden designers took their themes from sentimental verses about the moon and the wind, and from poems "composed over a cup of wine." The result was the emergence of "garden of landscape" or "garden of the literati." The Wangchuan Villa built for the Tang poet Wang Wei (700-760), for instance, was located in a natural valley mantled in green.

After the Yuan and Ming dynasties (1280-1644), small-scale gardens and courtyards came into being. These gardens occupied less space and were designed with a literary flavour, giving people the feeling that they were experiencing a large garden in miniature.

Figure 0-1 Efang Palace, situated in the suburbs of present-day Xi'an, Shaanxi Province, is one of the early imperial gardens in China. Construction work began in 212 B.C., but the palace was destroyed by fire in wars before it was completed. It extended 2.5 kilometres from east to west and over 1,000 paces from north to south. The front palace was built on a terrace 10 m in height, and could seat 10,000 people. There was enough space in front of the palace for 1,000 flagstaffs. Vestiges of the ruined palace are still extant. Here is part (approximately one-sixth) of a painting of Efang Palace by Yuan Wentao, an 18th-century court artist.

Figure 0-1

Figure 0-2   The Summer Palace, located in the western suburbs of Beijing, is an imperial garden which served as a temporary, imperial palace outside the capital. It was built in 1153 and was rebuilt in 1888. The garden covers an area of 290 hectares with the Longevity Hill as the centre of attraction. On the shoulder of the hill are groups of buildings with the Cloud-Dispelling Hall and the Fragrance of Buddha Pavilion standing on the central axis. The more than 700-m-long decorated wooden walkway stretches along the back of the Kunming Lake. Scattered around the lake are also pavilions, bridges, corridors and docks. At the back of the hill are age-old trees and elegant bamboo groves. Xie Qu Yuan (the Garden of Harmonious Interest) is "a garden within a garden." In the west appears a long dike and distant mountains.

Figure 0-2

Figure 0-3   Chengde Mountain Resort
Hebei Province. Construction began
1703 and was completed in 1790. It
the summer resort of the Qing
mperors.
   The resort, composed of a summer
alace and a garden, is enclosed by a
-kilometre-long wall. There are 72
enic spots. Shown here is one of them
amed the "Pagoda of Smoke and Rain."

Figure 0-3

13

Most of the centuries-old gardens in southern Jiangsu, Guangdong and Guangxi provinces belong to this type (Fig. 0-4).

The import of Buddhism also had a strong influence on Chinese garden design. When monks built their mountain temples, they made full use of the surrounding mountain scenery. Thus another kind of garden gradually evolved with a religious character. There is an old Chinese saying: "Monks have occupied most of the famous mountains under heaven."

II. Arrangement of Plantings in Traditional Chinese Gardens

Plants, as an important natural component of the garden, must be selected to enhance both the design of the garden and its artistic style. The main considerations in the arrangement of plantings are as follows:

1. The Artistic Effects of Trees.

An artistic illusion of forest can be created in a garden by grouping three or five big trees in a small area. This type of planting is often used in cities. It is not suitable for imperial gardens because there is enough space there to plant a real forest. The Wan Shu Yuan (Garden of Ten Thousand Trees) and Li Hua Yu (Flowering Pear-Tree Valley) in the imperial mountain retreat Bi Shu Shan Zhuang in Chengde are examples. Temples were often built in the woods to create the same effect.

Landscape designers often direct attention to the beauty of a massed grouping, sometimes concentrating on the cultivation of one variety of plant with a special characteristic. Examples of such gardens built in suitable natural environment are the Chinese Rose Garden, Peony Pavilion, Chinese Parasol Yard, Sunken Bed of Chinese Flowering Crabapple and Purple Water Caltrop Island found in some of the well-known gardens in China.

2. The Meaning of Plants.

Very often attention is focused on the beauty of a single plant. From ancient times, artists and scholars have used nature as the theme of their works. Plants change in accordance with the seasons and their environment, and these changes are often the source of inspiration for painters and poets. Sometimes the shape or the name of a plant lends itself to metaphor. For example, the peony signifies affluence because of its large, showy flower. The Chinese name for sweet osmanthus is *guihua*, the character *gui* has a homonym meaning high rank. So people grow peony and osmanthus together in a garden or at home to signify wealth and honour.

Sometimes plants are personified. The plum blossom is likened to a hardy, lone man because it is the only flower blooming in chilly early spring. Growing tall and straight, the bamboo symbolizes integrity. Because the orchid grows in quiet valleys it exemplifies simple elegance. The chrysanthemum blooms in defiance of autumn frost, signifying composure. Grown together, therefore, plum, bamboo, orchid, and chrysanthemum are personalized as the "four men of virtue." As another example, when pine, bamboo, and plum are planted in the same garden, they are called the "three winter friends" because pine and bamboo are green throughout the year and plum can blossom in the snow. Although this kind of personification is somewhat subjective, it gives pleasure to people as an artistic abstraction and is believed to shape their personality and raise their appreciative ability.

3. Coordinating Grounds and Buildings.

Appropriate plantings, especially when tied in with the metaphorical meanings of the plants, can increase the attraction of a building and make it more meaningful. For example, if several clumps of bamboo are planted near a study in a courtyard, visitors are given a sense of quiet and elegance. At the same time, the bamboo signifies the devotion of the owner to his study. Some buildings are named poetically for the plants surrounding them, such as Lotus Root Pavilion and Magnolia Hall. An ancient Chinese poem gives a vivid description of plum blossoms:

Several blooming plums stand in the shadow of a corner,
Their branches weighed down by clusters of snow.
A waft of fragrance from the distance
Gives away the indomitable flowers below.

III. Chinese Gardens Today

Today's gardens in China have inherited the traditional Chinese styles mentioned above and also absorbed foreign techniques. The art of garden design is constantly evolving. In the course of this evolution, however, the essence of the traditional Chinese garden—a tradition that is loved by the Chinese people—has remained intact.

The chief characteristics of Chinese garden design, from ancient times to the present, can be described as follows:

1. A natural grove is created with several trees. Equidistance is avoided.

2. Prominence is given to a special variety of tree to create "a wood in town."

3. The lawn is made to stretch in undulation. It may be embellished with stones signifying hills or with other decorations.

4. A path is cut through woods, bamboo clumps, or flowering shrubs instead of being lined with trees.

5. Trees in a courtyard with buildings are planted symmetrically while being kept in a natural state in other areas.

6. Certain patterns are observed in plant selection and combinations, depending on the intention of the designer. Some patterns have metaphorical significance, for example "three winter friends," "four men of virtue," or "red peach and green willow." Some express traditional concepts about plants, such as using locust trees to shelter a courtyard, bamboo to screen windows, or a pine to indicate welcome. These traditional patterns have become very familiar with the public over the years.

7. Most of the time, plants are kept natural, without pruning.

8. Emphasis is placed on arrangement of the plants according to the natural terrain. This is designed always to give visitors a pleasant surprise when they think they have come to a dead end—"Another hamlet suddenly came in sight, where the willows were dense and the flowers bright," to quote a great Tang poet.

This book will discuss, through examples, the relationship between different plants, and between plants and other design factor such as paths, stones, water and architectures in the landscaping of gardens, as well as the treatment of flower beds and the planting of courtyards. The author hopes that the book will give the reader a greater understanding of the principles of design underlying the traditional Chinese garden.

Figure 0-4

Figure 0-4 Most private gardens in ancient China were built in the south of the Jiangsu Province, especially in Suzhou and Yangzhou. Here is a garden in Suzhou. It is exquisitely designed with natural features.

Garden Plantings

Chapter One

Garden Plantings

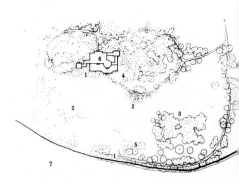

A garden is mainly composed of plants arranged for both artistic and functional purposes.

Garden plantings are different from buildings. The latter are artificial and fixed once they are completed, but the former belong to the natural world and change with time, locality and condition. The changes sometimes take hundreds of years to be perceived and sometimes take only a few days.

Figure 1-1 a

Garden plantings are neither natural forests or grasslands, nor man-made vegetations such as a shelter belt. They are natural plants artistically arranged by man to serve ornamental and practical purposes and, together with other features, create a healthful and enjoyable environment.

The vegetation in a garden is often made up of plants sensitive to seasonal changes which are reflected in the colour and appearance of their trunks, leaves, flowers and fruits, and their ecological forms are determined by temperature, humidity, soil and climate. So the garden designer must take into account all these characteristics, and carefully handle their interactions to give full expression to their beauty.

The following presentations and analyses focus on the composition of a vegetation, the central feature of a vegetation, the composition of trees, the colours and seasonal features of the plants and the ground arrangements.

I. Composition of a Vegetation

Like other artistic creations, the plant arrangements in a garden are first of all determined by the preconceived ideas and purposes of the designer. A scenery or an environment with a specific appeal is often achieved by the combination of a rich variety of plants with topography, particularly the landform. The process may begin with drawing up a plan showing the forest boundary and the canopy outline (the multi-dimensional contour line of forests or groves).

The perspective of a garden vegetation is chiefly determined by the proportion between the height of trees, the size of the lawn and the position of the sightseer.

A broad open space not only provides convenience for public activities but also gives a wide field of vision, suggesting spaciousness and broadness of mind. Figure 1-1b is an example of such a garden lawn with an area of 35,000 m^2. It is 130 m wide. The proportion between the height of trees and the width of the lawn is 1:10, enough to achieve the purpose of the designer. Figure 1-2b illustrates a 16,400-m^2-lawn slightly tilting northward toward the water. It is 150 m in breadth decorated by sedate and towering cedars and wayside southern magnolia. Viewed from the lower end of the slope, the cedars look even taller, straighter and more magnificent. However, the feeling of broadness is not always created by the sheer size of space. The vegetation showed in figure 1-3b only covers 4,080 m^2, still, it looks very imposing. This is achieved by surrounding it with a single variety of tree, and in this case, by sawtooth oak sparingly interspersed with Chinese sweetgums and camphor trees. Thus the canopy outline appears more uniform and the forest boundary line, more straightened out, giving greater depth to the landscape. With no trees across the lawn,

Figure 1-1 b

Figure 1-1   Lawn with a broad field of vision.

a. Plan: 1. Weeping willows. 2. Camphor trees. 3. Woods of Chinese wingnut and black locust. 4. Southern magnolia. 5. Deodar cedar. 6. Listen-to-the-Orioles Hall. 7. Lake

b. The lawn viewed from the south.

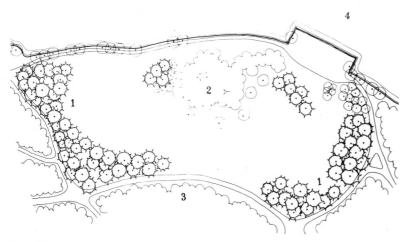

Figure 1-2 a

Figure 1-2

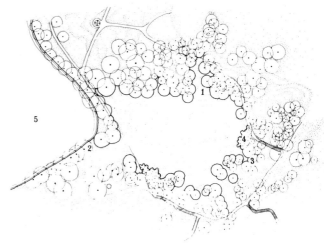

Figure 1-3 a

Figure 1-3 b

Figure 1-2 Lawn with groves of deodar cedar.

a. Plan: 1. Deodar cedars. 2. Woods of osmanthus and miscellaneous trees. 3. Southern magnolia. 4. Water surface.

b. Cedars at the northwest corner of the lawn. These towering cedars outline and accent the lawn.

the space appears neat and uninterrupted. It should be added that the lawn lies in a hollow surrounded by hillocks in the north, east and south, and slightly slants toward a body of water in the west. The straight and tall sawtooth oaks on the hillocks spread upward in even gradation on the slope until they are 35 m above the water area. Thus, with the help of the slope and the surrounding trees, the 170-meter-long lawn appears larger than its size.

These examples illustrate the appropriate utilization of topographical factors, woods and other landscape features such as extensive water surface, richly vegetated mountainsides, and so on. For trees, it is better to choose the tall ones with large crowns. Less tree variety would result in clear-cut canopy lines and create an air of wholeness. On the edges of an open space, it is advisable to plant the trees at random instead of in solid groves to enhance depth of view. In the central part of the open space, it is inadvisable to plant trees in too many layers. Thus, the layout as a whole would achieve broadness of view through the interaction of height, breadth, depth and wholeness.

In creating a closed-in vegetation, the area should be smaller and surrounded by layers of dense groves, leaving some narrow openings so that the sightseer can enjoy the scenery beyond.

For example, consider a garden with an area of only 200 m². Densely planted on its edges are tobira pittosporum and Chinese juniper, forming a 2-metre-high hedgerow (figure 1-4). Scattered near the hedgerows are camphor trees, glossy privets, Japanese maples, Chinese parasol trees and other arboreal plantings, making the hedgerows thicker and more interesting. Crapemyrtles are planted at the entrance of the garden, with groups of camphor trees near the centre and seats underneath. Here, the sightseer can enjoy the mountain scenery in the distance through the openings from a closed-in and quiet spot.

However, a garden designer more often aims at creating gardens for special purposes. For instance, to meet the urban people's desire for natural scenery, some parts of the city with moderate slopes may be used to create a "mountain forest" within walking distance. Figure 1-5 is a hillside lawn in a city in south China. The area is 5,680 m² with an elevation of only five metres. The whole area is divided by a ridge into two areas facing south and west respectively.

Scanning the lawn from the south, one sees dense bamboo groves on one side and sparse woods on the other. A pavilion and its veranda barely visible through the woods enhance the feeling of depth. The groves on the slope are only 15 m in depth interspersed at random with camphor trees, Chinese parasols, locust trees and glossy privets. Lower on the slope are turf, and underneath the trees are shade-tolerant shrubs. The path on the slope is only 1 m wide, shaded by trees with crowns of more than 20 m in diameter. The arrangement of plantings on the whole hides the actual elevation of the garden and creates an environment resembling a forest deep in the mountains.

Looking at the lawn from the west, one sees a group of apricot trees planted at random, the branches inclining in the same direction as the slope. Viewed from the foot of the hill, the tilting crowns of the apricot trees seem to enlarge the area of the woods. In blossoming season, tiers of apricot flowers on the slope present a very charming aura of "Spring in the air with apricots strewn with flowers in silver pink" as was aptly depicted by an ancient Chinese poet. The turf stretches up to the top of the undulating slope as if the grounds were heaving in gentle green waves.

Temple gardens designed for a different purpose require to be more integrated with natural vegetation. They are usually located in deep forests to be seclusive as most temples are (figure 1-6).

Sometimes the natural woods surrounding a temple are interplanted with groves of oriental sweetgums to tinge the forests with patches of red leaves (figure 1-7). Such semi-natural vegetation plan is another expression of the Chinese concept of an "ancient

Figure 1-3 A vegetation screened off by trees.

a. Plan: 1. Sawtooth oaks. 2. Weeping willows. 3. Oriental sweetgums. 4. Broadleaf sasa. 5. Lake.

b. The green screen formed by thick groves of sawtooth oak.

temple tucked away in the mountains."

The next step in designing a garden is the determination of the forest boundary, or the continuous line delineating the vertical projection of the crowns at the boundary of a forest or a grove as it is cast by the sunlight at mid-day. As the design of a forest boundary reflects the arrangement of plantings on the ground, it is an important method to plan the spatial division of a garden. The space required, the depth of vision, the perspective line and the creation of atmosphere depend mostly on the design of forest boundary. This concept can also be applied to creating a small space amid a large one. For example, to build a small space in a wood, low shrubs can be planted around a chosen grove, forming a closed-in space like an "inner room" in a big house. Here, the sightseer can enjoy an unexpected scenic spot different from the rest of the woods. Figure 1-8 shows a small shaded space of this type with densely planted flower shrubs around a grove of trident maples.

Forest boundaries are pertinent to adapting the topography of spaces of equal areas and similar shapes to the surrounding environment, resulting in vegetation plans of different formations, functions and interests. The areas of the four lawns in figure 1-9 are all about 2,200-2,500 m². But they generate varied interests due to the employment of different designs of forest boundary lines. Lawns a. and b. both form a semi-open space with plants. Lawn b. faces a fish pond and lawn a., a vegetation with ornamental flowers. The short forest boundary lines enhance spaciousness of the lawns. Lawn c. tilts from the north to the south. The forest boundary line is elongated from south to north and short from east to west, thus increasing the effect of the slope. But for lawn d., the central part is slightly elevated, creating a gradual hump. Its surrounding areas are densely planted with southern magnolias and trident maples to form a completely closed-in space with short boundaries. The setting brings tranquility and turns the elevation in the centre of the lawn into just another open space in the woods.

Curved forest boundary lines can serve to increase the depth of vision. In figure 1-3, for instance, if the forest boundary north of the lawn is not made so straight but curved, the trees would appear in more layers, and the shady area would be extended to protect the sightseers from the heat of a setting sun in summertime.

The space division of a garden is also achieved through the design of the canopy lines, namely, the contour formed by the foliage of the trees. The forest boundary line alone cannot fully indicate the spatial aspect of a vegetated garden, because trees vary in height and branch point. The canopy lines show these dimensions which have a direct bearing on the field of vision and spatial appeal. When the plants or the tree crowns block the sight, the sightseer would have a feeling of seclusion; when they do not, they would become part of a broader view.

Arrangements of trees with the same height can form a straight, plain but imposing canopy line and give expression to the beautiful shape of a particular kind of tree, such as the straightness of deodar cedars or the softness of willows. The grouping of trees with different height creates a wavy and varied canopy line. In a vegetation on flat grounds, the canopy line should be made to rise and fall in a rhythmic flow and reflect the seasonal changes of colour. Figure 1-10 shows the variegated canopy lines made up of many different shrubs and arboreal plants, increasing the spatial beauty of the vegetation. Sometimes a single high tree rears over a grove of lower ones like a "crane standing among chickens," as a Chinese saying goes, which can serve as a landmark for sightseers (figure 1-11).

The design of a canopy line should be closely adapted to the topography. When the surface of the ground is uneven, the canopy line will rise and dip even if the plants are of the same height. The growth rate of different trees and the characteristics of various deciduous and evergreen trees can also bring about many changes to the canopy lines. All this must be taken into careful consideration in garden making.

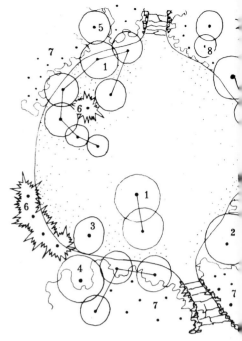

Figure 1-4 a

Figure 1-5 a

Figure 1-4 A closed-in vegetation.

a. Plan: The closed-in space has an entrance and an exit with occasional openings. The trees are mainly: 1. Camphor tree. 2. Oriental plane tree. 3. Japanese maple. 4. Chinese parasol. 5. Crapemyrtle. 6. Chinese juniper. 7. Tobira pittosporum. 8. Glossy privet.

b. From the tranquility of the bench, one can get glimpses of the scenery beyond the closed-in space through openings in the surrounding woods.

Figure 1-4 b

Figure 1-5 A vegetation with the area of a mountain forest.

a. Plan: 1. A grove of apricot trees. 2. Glossy privet Ait and other trees. 3. Bamboo groves. 4. Camphor trees and osmanthus groves. 5. Large camphor trees. 6. Oriental plane trees.

b. A slope across the lawn with various kinds of trees, creating depth and increasing the effect of a mountain forest.

Figure 1-5 b

Figure 1-6

Figure 1-6 The scenery of a Buddhist temple deep in a mountain forest.

25

Besides the canopy line, the height of the branch points produces different spatial effects.

In general, there is more space under arboreal plants, but this is not so under southern magnolias, young sweet osmanthus and Chinese photinia. The branch points of some coniferous trees like the deodar cedar, lovely golden larch and metasequoia are so low that the sightseer cannot go under their crowns. The branch points of the masson pine and Japanese black pine are high, so the sightseer can rest under their shades. All this shows that the spatial effects created by canopy lines and forest boundaries are varied according to the varieties, ages and forms of the trees, the ways they are pruned as well as climatic changes and topographic features. It is up to the designer to choose the canopy lines and forest boundaries best suited to the purpose of the garden.

Figure 1-7

Figure 1-7   Oriental sweetgums with red leaves, setting off the ancient temple.

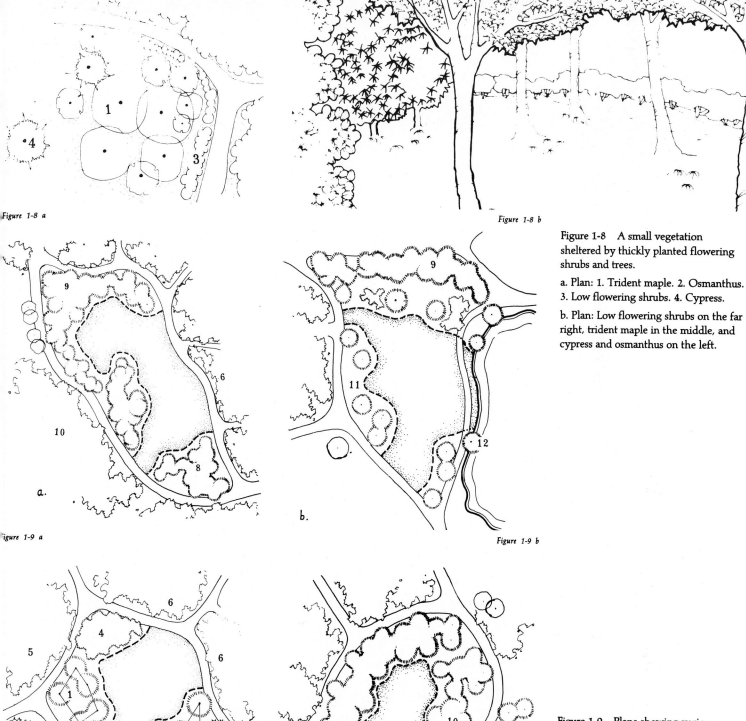

Figure 1-8 a

Figure 1-8 b

Figure 1-9 a

Figure 1-9 b

Figure 1-9 c

Figure 1-9 d

Figure 1-8   A small vegetation sheltered by thickly planted flowering shrubs and trees.

a. Plan: 1. Trident maple. 2. Osmanthus. 3. Low flowering shrubs. 4. Cypress.

b. Plan: Low flowering shrubs on the far right, trident maple in the middle, and cypress and osmanthus on the left.

Figure 1-9   Plans showing various forest boundary designs.

a. and b. Open vegetations. c. A slanting vegetation. d. A closed-in vegetation. Major tree varieties: 1. Silk tree. 2. Oriental plane tree. 3. Cypress. 4. Flowering shrub. 5. Trident maple. 6. Low flowering shrub. 7. Cherry tree. 8. Evergreen arboreous trees. 9. Deciduous arboreous trees. 10. Southern magnolia. 11. Crapemyrtle. 12. Weeping willow.

Figure 1-10

Figure 1-10　Canopy outlines formed
by different trees and shrubs.

Figure 1-11

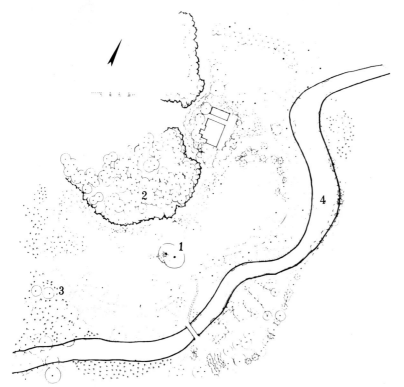

Figure 1-12 a

Figure 1-12 b

Figure 1-13 b

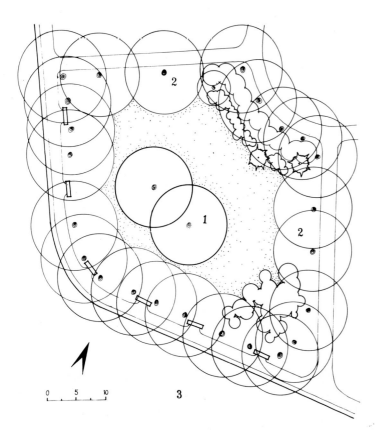

Figure 1-13 a

Figure 1-14

Figure 1-14   Sketch: A vegetation with shrubs as its major scenic interest.

Figure 1-11   A design giving prominence to the canopy outline of an isolated tree (Japanese cinnamon).

Figure 1-12   A vegetation featuring a major scene.

. Plan: 1. Oriental sweetgums. 2. Evergreen groves. 3. Bamboo groves. 4. Stream.

. The two oriental sweetgums as the major scenic feature stress the autumn aura of the space.

Figure 1-13   Dominant trees in a fan-shaped vegetation.

. Plan: 1. Chinese soapberry trees. 2. Oriental plane trees. 3. Lake.

. Sketch: The two Chinese soapberries viewed from a distance.

II. Central Feature of a Vegetation

A garden vegetation usually has a major attraction which is often composed of trees with special decorative value. Figure 1-12 is a vegetation covering an area of 7,900 m². Two 30-metre-high oriental sweetgums stand side by side in the middle of the kidney-shaped lawn. In autumn, their red leaves are conspicuously symbolic of the season. The two trees as the centre piece of the lawn enhance the depth of the view. The space in figure 1-13 fans out toward the water with two 9-metre-high Chinese soapberry trees in the centre as the major attraction. The trees are 7 m apart, with umbrella-shaped crowns providing a 300-m² shady area. The pinnate leaves are green in summer and light-yellow in autumn, and the trunks are in light grey. The height under the crown is 5 m, allowing a wide field of vision. Seats are set under the trees with a restful view of the green rippling lake.

Some vegetations take a tract of shrubs as their major feature. Figure 1-14 is an example with a 30-metre-wide grove of 40 big leave hydrangeas planted at random on a medium-sized lawn against a backdrop of big arboreal trees such as the *Phoebe sheareri* and the ginkgo. When in full bloom in April, they form a magnificent scene. There is a forest of white common lilacs as one of the major plantings in Beijing's Tiantan Park (Temple of Heaven Park) (figure 1-15). In the blossoming season, the wide spread of lilac is a sea of small white flowers sending forth delicate fragrance.

A vegetation sometimes has flower beds as its major attraction. The centre of interest in the lawn in figure 1-16 is composed of seasonal flower beds, a pavilion and a rockery. Although in dimension the pavilion is dwarfed by the southern magnolias and the yulan magnolias by its side, it is situated on a 2-metre-high rockery group and blends well with the surrounding arboreal plants and shrubs which blossom by turns the whole year round. Together, they form an outstanding feature in the garden.

In brief, when using plants as the major attraction, such as a single tree, two "sister trees," a grove or a small garden with flower beds, plants, rockery and buildings, they should be eye-catching and attractive from more than one angle. If it is a single tree, it should be handsome and long-lived, and fairly big with bright luxuriant foliage, such as a locust tree, a ginkgo, a deodar cedar, an oriental sweetgum, a camphor tree, a Chinese soapberry tree or a banyan tree.

The designer of a traditional Chinese garden often resorts to the art of gradually leading the sightseer to a scenery instead of exposing it all at once. This is a good approach in planning the major feature of a vegetation. Figure 1-17 is one such example on the bank of the famous West Lake in Hangzhou. It covers an area of about 2,800 m², bordering the water on the north and sheltered from a road on the south by a thick row of trees, forming a tranquil lawn. Thirteen weeping willows stand at varying intervals along the bank of the lake, providing natural shadowy space. The forest boundaries and the canopy lines in the space are rather plain and the colours are soft, but the scene is fascinating. There are several contributing factors. The lawn gradually slants from the south toward the lake in the north. Through the gaps between the trees on the bank, one can see the Sudi Causeway extending across the water surface. And between the causeway and the trees, one can faintly see "Three Pools Mirroring the Moon" and the distant view of the Liu Village Garden, presenting a scene of "dyke beyond dyke and water beyond water." With the advent of autumn, the red foliage of Java bishop woods of the Sudi Causeway set against the bluish-green mountainside in the distance deepens the field of vision. However, this panoramic view does not meet the eyes all at once. When the sightseer walks the lawn from the east or west, the main attractions are the shady willows on the lakeside. As he rambles towards the trees and comes closer and closer to the waterfront, the field of vision gradually expands until the bank is reached. Then the beautiful scenery of West Lake comes into full view. Here the 13 willows play a prelusory role. The design of the lakeside lawn aptly exemplifies the art of enhancing the sightseer's interest through step-by-step revelation of the major scenery.

Figure 1-15

Figure 1-15   Sketch: A vegetation in Beijing's Temple of Heaven Park featuring a grove of lilacs surrounded by ancient cypresses.

III. Composition of Trees

There are generally several ways to arrange the trees in a garden.

Composition of woods. A wooded tract with tall trees of single variety freely planted will form a shady vegetation and add to the feeling of being in the "woods" (figure 1-18a). It is particularly desirable to choose trees with characteristics that can create a scene of "a wood in the city." A method often used in city gardens is to choose trees with strong seasonal appeal. A woody vegetation is mainly achieved by close planting. First, it is important to make use of topographical undulation and set it off with rockery, low shrubs and paths. The contrasts in the height and size of these embellishments will heighten the atmosphere of a woodland. Secondly, it requires thick shade with a coverage rate of about 90%. So large arboreal trees are usually preferred to shrubs (figure 1-18b). The trees are usually planted at random to create an aura of wilderness. Orderly planting patterns should be used less in gardens of this type.

Composition of trees. The trees can be of a single variety (figure 1-19a) or of several varieties (figure 1-19b). The choice, quantity and spacing of trees mainly depend on the purpose of the designer, including aesthetic and functional considerations, and the environment. Using a single kind of tree is relatively easier than using more than one kind. In the latter case, special attention should be paid to the changes in shape and colour of different trees in different seasons as well as to the artistic effects of layers and backgrounds. For instance, a single tree, a tree of colourful leaves or a flowering tree blends well with high groves in the background. One grove can also serve as the background of another grove (figure 1-20).

The following guidelines are offered for the spacing of trees in groves.

1. Functional Requirements.

If the space should be of a closed-in type, it is better to have the tree crowns touching each other. The spacing should be determined by the largest crown diameter of different trees during their steady growing periods. If it is desired to have a shady space for activities, big arboreal trees planted at 5 m to 15 m intervals are preferable. For playing chess in the shades, the trees should be at least 5 m apart and the seats, 3 m apart.

2. Biological Characteristics.

Figure 1-16

Figure 1-16   A garden scene composed of flower beds, rockeries and a pavilion.

Figure 1-17   A vegetation designed to enhance the sightseer's interest step by step.

a. Plan: 1. Weeping willows. 2. Chinese junipers and tobira pittosporum forming a shelterbelt. 3. Crapemyrtle. 4. Lake.

b. 13 weeping willows provide shade without blocking the sight.

c. As the sightseer walks down the slope toward the lake, his vision gradually broadens until he gains a full view of the lake and the scenery on the opposite bank from under the willows.

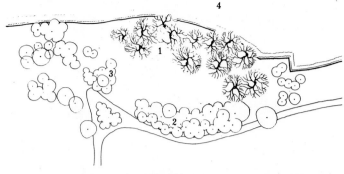

Figure 1-17 a

Figure 1-17 b

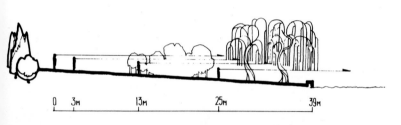

0   3M   13M   25M   39M

Figure 1-17 c

Figure 1-18 a

Figure 1-18   Creating a woodland atmosphere.

a. A forest of ancient cypresses with thick shade.

b. A forest of oriental plane trees.

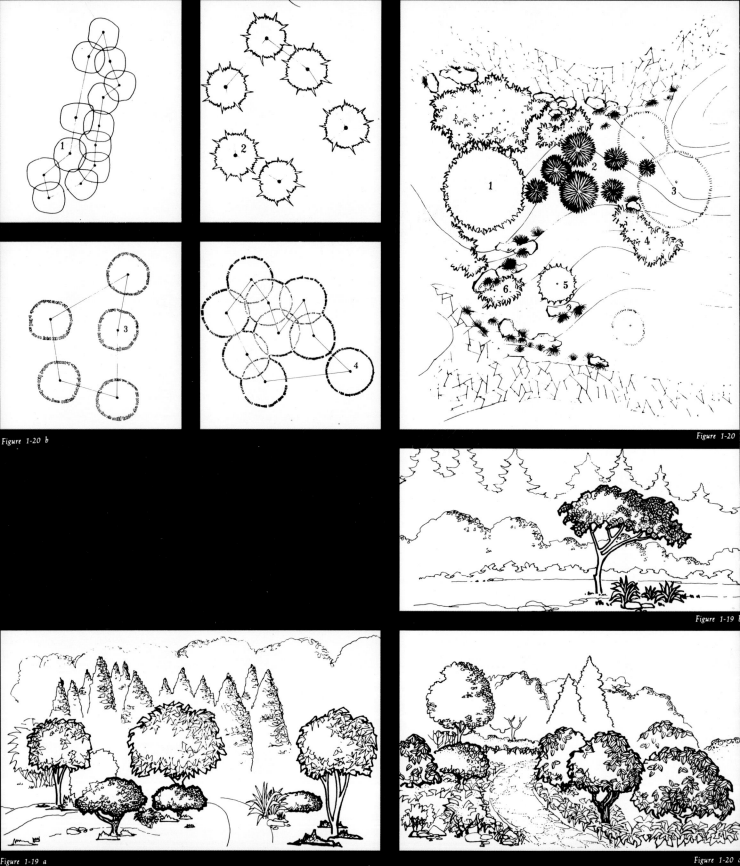

Figure 1-20 b

Figure 1-20

Figure 1-19 b

Figure 1-19 a

Figure 1-20

Figure 1-19   Plans for groves of trees.

1. With single kind of trees: 1. Weeping willow. 2. Deodar cedar. 3. Silk tree. 4. Oriental plane tree.

2. With multiple kinds of trees: 1. lacebark pine. 2. Flowering pineapple. 3. Japanese maple. 4. Bamboo. 5. Chinese juniper. 6. Sargent Chinese juniper.

In determining the distances between trees, it is necessary to reserve enough space for their crowns when they reach their maximum dimension in the steady-growth period, taking into consideration the growth rate of different types of trees. Special attention should be paid to the different characteristics of sun plants and cold-tolerant and shade-tolerant plants so that they do not interfere with each other's growth. For instance, cherry trees are direly afraid of scorching heat, and when planted in the warm south, the space between the trees should be narrower so that they can give shade to each other. Peach trees, however, like sunlight, so they should be spaced at larger intervals and there should be no big trees nearby that block the sun.

3. Aesthetic Requirements.

Natural appeal should be stressed with thin and dense areas alternated in proper perspective, avoiding straight visual lines. The characteristics of the heights, sizes, colours and shapes of different trees should be considered for achieving coherence with the surrounding environment.

4. Economic Benefits and Saving of Plant Materials.

If two trees can meet the design requirement, three will be superfluous. Rare trees and those with high ornamental value should be arranged at the edge or placed where the sightseer can take a close look at them.

In the light of these guidelines, the following general criteria are offered for reference in figuring the distances between groves.

Small broadleaf arboreal plants like osmanthus and yulan magnolias: 3 to 8 m.

Large broadleaf arboreal plants like plane trees and camphor trees: 5 to 15 m.

Small coniferous arboreal plants like the Japanese white pine and yew podocarpus: 2 to 5 m.

Large coniferous trees like the Chinese pine and deodar cedar: 7 to 18 m.

Flowering shrubs: 1 to 5 m.

In short, the distance between the trees is flexible, depending on the design requirements, the characteristics of the trees and topography.

Composition of a tree belt. The tree belt is mainly used for background, serving as a separation device or a shield. Tree belts with a single kind of tree often take the form of a high hedge looking like a green wall. Composed of different trees, it often has many layers. Figure 1-21a shows a separation belt between the lawn and the main path in a garden. The hedge is 5 m thick, extending 40 m. Since the trees constitute part of the view on both sides, they are arranged in several layers.

Layer 1. Edible canna, 1.2 m in height at 0.5 m intervals.

Layer 2. Evergreen tobira pittosporum, 1.5 m in height at 1 to 1.5 m interval.

Layer 3. Evergreen Chinese juniper with low branch point, 3 to 4 m in height at 2 m interval.

Layer 4. Cherry trees, 3 m in height, at 2.5 to 3 m interval. The distance between the different layers is 1 to 2 m.

Figure 1-20   Sketches of background trees.

a. Backgrounding in 3 layers: a single silk tree with deodar cedars in the distance as its background. Low trees and shrubs are grown in-between as accents.

b. Backgrounding in 4 layers: 3 trunks of faber maple serve as the background of the low arboreous trees in the foreground. The deodar cedars, which are the background for the maples and the willow trees in the distance, serve the same function for the cedars.

c. Groves as background: A grove of low round-shaped trees take the cone-shaped tree groves as background. The latter form an interesting contrast with the adjacent high ball-shaped arboreous trees.

Looking from the lawn, the red flowers of the cannas are set against the emerald green tobira pittosporum and the dark green Chinese juniper. Looking from the main path, the row of junipers serve as a backdrop for the cherry blossoms when they are in full bloom. Here the tall junipers serve a double purpose. Figure 1-21b shows a belt-grove planted along a wall. It is mainly composed of evergreen fortunes windmill palms and slenderer lady palms, which are both of high ornamental value.

For background, it is better to use a single kind of tree to produce a uniform style and a clean canopy line. If different kinds of trees are used, it is preferable to choose those similar in height, form and crown shape. When the background is composed of a tract of trees, it is advisable to use mixed trees of different crown shapes, heights and colours, but they should not be higher than the general canopy line so as to avoid the secondary overshadowing the primary. For a belt, it is better to plant the trees at closer intervals or stagger them in double rows. When arranged in tracts, the trees at the edge should be planted closer, but those inside should be sparse to allow better ventilation and lighting. In brief, the composition of background groves should be dense, forming a complete and compact green wall to set off the front scene. Also, the background trees must be higher than those in the front, and it is better to choose those evergreen arbour or shrub plants which are darkish in colour, branchy and leafy with low branch points, and have dense canopies and indistinct flowers, such as the evergreen sweet viburnum, the Chinese juniper, the tobira pittosporum and the weeping willow.

Figure 1-21 a

Composition with one tree: As it has been said before, a single tree is often the major attraction, but more often it is planted for shade, in which case it should have a large canopy of 2.5-3.5 m above ground, have dense and broad leaves and be pest-free (figure 1-22a). The shade trees often seen in China include locust tree, weeping willow, hackberry, Chinese soapberry, oriental plane tree, camphor tree, buckeye, sawtooth oak, banyan tree, Chinese redbud, silkoak grevillea, flamboyant tree and bo tree.

When choosing shade trees, attention should be paid to their shapes, ages and the ways they are pruned. Trees with spherical or umbrella-shaped crowns have better shade effects than those in the shape of a cylinder or a cone. The young cedar tapers to an apex and hardly gives any shade. However, with proper pruning, it can become a very good shade tree in 30 or 40 years.

It is preferable to leave a broad space around a single shade tree with few shrubs and flowers within the shady area, so as to avoid blocking the sightseer's line of vision. Often a sturdy ancient single tree that has survived over the centuries not only offers shade but also serves as the main attraction in the surrounding area. Figure 1-22b shows an ancient banyan tree on the bank of the picturesque Lijiang River in Guangxi. The gnarled old tree with rich foliage spreading over an area of more than 700 m² is said to be over 1,300 years old.

An ancient poet wrote the following lines in praise of the tree:

An eye-feasting wonder for halcyon voyagers on the boat,
A much-needed shade for sweating travellers on the road.
Around its gnarled trunk endless vines twine,
Like ancient dragons revived in a land of gold.

IV. Colours and Seasonal Features of the Plants

Different plants have different scenic values. They vary in stance, and their trunks have different colours such as yellow, brown, dark brown and greyish-white, and their barks show different vertical and horizontal patterns. Their fruits also come in various shapes, sizes, colours and flavours. All these are important elements in garden making, the most effective are the shapes of the flowers, leaves, and their colours which create seasonal features. Displaying plant colours for maximum effect requires meticulous arrangement.

Most plant leaves are green, but the colours vary in degree. Some are light, some dark, other may turn into another colour in time. The colours usually change with the four seasons. For instance at the sprouting of the weeping willows, the leaves are yellowish-green

Figure 1-22 a

Figure 1-21 b

Figure 1-21   Plants in belt.

a. A sheltering belt in two layers composed of tobira pittosparum, Chinese juniper, cherry tree and others.

b. A sheltering belt composed of palms and slenderer ladypalms between the road and the wall.

Figure 1-22   Disposition of single trees used to present a picturesque scene or to provide shade in an otherwise shadeless open space.

a. An artificially planted hackberry tree whose large canopy offers excellent shade.

b. A single natural banyan tree without other trees around it.

and they gradually turn to light green and dark green in summer and autumn. Besides green leaves, there are also yellow, red and purple ones, such as the purple leaves of the purpleleaf plum and the red leaves of the maple. In spring the ginkgo and Chinese sapium leaves are green but in autumn the former turn yellow and the latter become red. The leaves of the Japanese maples turn from red to green in spring and back to red in autumn. These kinds of trees are generally called colour-leaf trees.

In the middle and lower reaches of the Changjiang (Yangtse) River in China, the four seasons are clearly divided, and the leaves undergo distinct colour changes. In other areas, though the seasonal division is not so distinct, there are also seasonal scenes enhanced by the local colour-leaf trees. Listed below are the major colour-leaf trees in the areas of Beijing and Shanghai:

Figure 1-22 b

IN BEIJING

Name of tree	Leaf form	Leaf Colour				Red leaf period	No. of days of the period
		Spring	Summer	Autumn	Winter		
Ginkgo	fan shape	yellow-ish green		yellow leafless	leafless	mid- Oct. to early Nov.	18-20
Chinese chestnut	lanceolate, simple alternate			yellow	ditto	late Oct. to early Nov.	11
Daimyo oak	inverted egg, alternate			yellow	ditto	mid- Oct. to late Oct.	19
Bigfruit elm	wide inverted egg, alternate			orange	ditto	mid- Oct. to late Oct.	17
Truncate-leaved maple	heavily serrated, opposite			reddish yellow	ditto	late Oct. to early Nov.	21
Chinese pistache	even pinnate, compound, alternate			red	ditto	mid- Oct. to early Nov.	21
Persimmon tree	oval, alternate			dark red	ditto	mid- Oct. to late Oct.	16
Korean ash	odd pinnate, compound, opposite			yellow	ditto	mid- Oct. to late Oct.	14
Smoke tree	round, alternate			fiery red	ditto	mid- Oct. to early Nov.	21
Chinese hawthorn	palmate (trifolio-late), alternate			orange red	ditto	late Oct. to early Nov.	12
Japanese creeper	palmate (trifolio-late), egg-shaped, alternate			orange red	ditto	early Oct. to late Oct.	21

Name of tree	Leaf form	Leaf Colour				Red leaf period	No. of days of the period
		Spring	Summer	Autumn	Winter		
Chinese soapberry	even pinnate, compound			yellow	leafless	early Nov. to early Dec.	25-30
Ginkgo	simple and in cluster			yellow	ditto	mid- Oct. to early Nov.	
Java bishopwood	alternate			brownish red	ditto	mid- Oct. to mid- Nov.	30
Oriental sweetgum	palmate (trifoliolate)			reddish yellow	ditto	Nov. to early Dec.	30
Trident maple				yellowy red	ditto	late Oct. to early Dec.	40
Chinese sapium	alternate			red	ditto	late Oct. to early Dec.	40
Faber maple		red	red	red	ditto	leaves fall in early Dec.	three seasons
Japanese maple	palmate (quinque-foliolate)			red	ditto		
Purpleleaf plum		dark red	dark red	dark red	ditto	leaves fall in mid- Dec.	three seasons
Camphor tree	alternately opposite	brownish red	green	green	green		
Sawtooth oak	alternate, serrate margin			brownish yellow	leafless	early Nov. to end of Nov.	30
Oriental plane tree	alternate, heavily serrated margin			yellow	ditto	mid- Nov. to early Dec.	20

Colour-leaf trees are generally arranged on the main body of a lawn to form a major scenic element or along the edges of a path or a lawn. Sometimes, they form a grove, presenting a beautiful mosaic of colour in autumn.

Since leaves have various shades of green which directly affect the colour pattern of a vegetation, the shades of green leaves are commonly divided into four grades as a guide to the disposition of plants.

Grade	Leaf colour	Tree types and representative trees
1	thin green	deciduous trees in spring, such as the willows.
2	light green	broad-leaf deciduous trees such as the oriental plane trees.
3	deep green	broad-leaf evergreens such as the camphor trees.
4	dark green	coniforous trees such as the cypress.

Naturally, the shades of green vary with trees, localities and seasons. For instance, southern magnolia shows a colour of shining dark green; ginkgo, light green and dragon spruce, greyish green. For the same kind of tree, the leaf colours may vary because of soil condition, temperature and humidity. For example, the leaves of cape jasmine are normally dark green, but change to yellow green if the soil lacks iron. The leaves of goldrain trees, camphor trees, ailanthus, and trident maple change from light to dark and back from dark to light along with the seasons. For some trees, the leaves are red at the time of sprouting or changing. The leaves of oriental plane tree, Canadian poplar and sawtooth oak turn golden before shedding. The shades of green also change in relation with light. When light is strong the colour appears thinner. Leaves with luster appear darker than those without. For instance, the leaves of camellia and osmanthus belong to the same colour grade, but the foliage colour of the former appears deeper than that of the latter.

Generally speaking, in handling leaf colours, clear contrast is preferable. For example, ginkgo and Chinese juniper produce a sharp contrast in leaf colour. However, there are other factors to be considered, too. The leaf colours of willow and camphor tree are similar, but they combine rather well because of their contrast in shape. The willow and ginkgo trees have similar leaf colours, but the ginkgo foliage looks darker in the sun because of its density, while the willows are loose-leaved and appear lighter in colour. Two more examples are the sargent Chinese juniper and the Japanese white pine. Although they have similar leaf colours, they are very different in shape: the former lies low and the branches stretch upward, while the latter's branches bend toward the ground and spread horizontally. Thus, the contrast in shape can divert attention from the leaf colour. So in considering the contrast of leaf colours, other characteristics of the trees should be taken into account at the same time.

The use of various shades of leaf and flower colours with a graded arrangement of trees and shrubs of different heights can produce a tiered pattern of rich colours. Figure 1-23 is a grove of many tiers of trees in deep green, light green, bright red and deep red. A path runs through the grove with dwarf lilyturf and the scarlet Indian azaleas covering the rockery and ground on both sides. The deep red Japanese maples stand at the back of the azaleas, with deep green cypress and lacebark pines as accents, revealing a small part of the light green oriental sweetgums at the far back. The proper arrangements of colours and shapes contribute considerably to the artistic appeal of the scene. The tiering of trees and shrubs of different colours is a common feature in garden designs and is mostly used in

Figure 1-23

Figure 1-23 Colour composition of plants planted in layers.
The scarlet azaleas match the dark red Japanese maples with dwarf lilyturf in the foreground and lacebark pines providing the background. At the far back are oriental sweetgums with their light green leaves matching the dark green pines.

opposite scenes along paths, at the edges of lawns, in front of large groves or in other prominent positions (figure 1-24).

In making garden designs of this type, attention should be paid to the colours at the time when there are no flowers, or when leaf colours have not yet changed, because this period lasts rather long. The common flowering shrubs only blossom 7-14 days, and the autumn colour leaves usually last only 2-4 weeks. The cut-leaved maple is exceptionally different. Its leaves are red in March and April, change to green in summer and turn red again in autumn. The tree is bare in winter. Such multiple colour changes should be given careful consideration in tree disposition. In the meantime, attention should be paid to height. In general, the height of trees should gradually increase between adjacent tiers. For better perspective, the height difference between the front rows should be smaller than between the tiers at the back.

The yearly changes in foliage and flowerage create different seasonal complexions of a vegetation. The usual way to accentuate the seasonal appeal is to choose a single kind or several kinds of trees or flowers and plant them in enough quantity to create a "climate" for the sightseer. For centuries, lovers of nature in China have followed the tradition of identifying seasons with flowers and trees. For instance, at the Mid-Autumn Festival they relish the osmanthus and in winter, the plum blossom. Figures 1-25 a-d contain a set of pictures showing plants with different seasonal features: a. cherry trees symbolic of spring; b. crapemyrtles, of summer; c. maples, of autumn and d. camellias, of winter.

However, although seasonal flowers or leaves are typical, the flowering periods or the changes in leaf colour last at most one to two months. Thus the periods should be methodically staggered so as to minimize the drab periods. In garden designs, the following methods are recommended:

1. Arrange in tiers plants of different flowering times. For instance, mixed with myrobalan plums and Japanese maples, the following flowering plants arranged in tiers can make the flowering time last for half a year: azalea (flowering from mid-April to early May), crapemyrtle (from early June to late June), Chinese St. Johnswort (from early June to early July), flowering pineapples (from late August to mid-September). In arranging the tiers, plants with longer flowering times should be given more space in width and thickness to enhance the effect. Flowering trees and shrubs of the same colour but different flowering periods can be arranged in successive tiers so that the colour scene would move up from tier to tier and last longer. When plants of the same flowering period but different colours are mixed in the same tier, a medley of colours would dominate the scene in different periods. However, this arrangement is mostly used in the blooming season or during holidays to create a special atmosphere.

2. Mix plants of different flowering times. Those with long flowering times and beautiful colours should be planted in larger numbers, in groves with successive waves of bloom throughout the flowering season. For example, the flowering period of a mixed vegetation of pomegranate, crapemyrtle and sweet-scented oleander can last five months. Plum trees remain in full bloom for less than two weeks, so they should be mixed with azalea which flower in spring, and crapemyrtle which blossom in summer, producing flowers for enjoyment over three seasons. In early winter, herbaceous flowers such as the scarlet sage or perennial herbaceous plants like the chrysanthemum scattered among groves of plum trees can help avoid flowerless periods.

3. Use herbaceous flowers to fill the gaps left by arboreal flowers. The perennial herbaceous flowering plants are widely diversified in species, colour and flowering period, and are therefore excellent for prolonging the overall blossoming season. For example, the cherry blossoms in full bloom are very attractive but short-lived. They last at most a week. The following planting scheme can be used to basically eliminate a withered appearance of

Figure 1-24 b

Figure 1-24 a

Figure 1-24 c

the vegetation:

First layer: striped marigold, height: 0.5 m, width: 1 m.

Second layer: aztec marigold, height: 0.5-1 m, width: 1-1.2 m.

Third layer: kochia, height: 0.8-1 m, width 0.3 to 0.4 m.

Forth layer: cherry trees, height: 1 to 2 m, width: 5 m (mixed with osmanthus).

Fifth layer: *Phoebe sheareri*, height: 10 m (mixed with ginkgo and oriental sweetgum).

The lengths of the five tiers mentioned in the above depend on the environment. In general, lengths of 20-30 m provide magnificent colour. When the cherry blossoms fade, the aztec marigold will form a wall of yellow flowers from June through August and set off the green kochia immediately behind. The layer of cherry trees, which are the major attraction, should outnumber the other trees. Although the cherry blossoms are of brief duration, the interplanted evergreen osmanthus and the evergreen *Phoebe sheareri* in the background mixed with ginkgoes and Chinese sweetgums combine to provide clumps of colourful flowers and leaves in three seasons and evergreens in winter.

If it is intended to give prominence to the seasonal feature of cherry blossoms at the edges of a wide vegetation or at out-of-the-way places without the embellishment of perennial flowering plants, the trees can then be planted in the midst of a thick layer of evergreen tobira pittosporums and weeping willows. When the cherry blossoms are in full bloom, the luxuriant flowerage would appear in the distance like floating clouds over a sea of green foliage.

Sometimes, it requires presentation of the four seasonal features in the same vegetation. The following example is a successful design to this end:

Figure 1-26 shows a relatively closed-in vegetation covering an area of 2,150 m². The ground slants from northwest to southeast and is surrounded by trees and shrubs. The major attraction is a grove of five silk trees planted on the highest part of the space. Facing them on the opposite side are nine oriental plane trees with a tract of cypress at the back. Some cherry trees are planted along the path on the southern edge of the space. In the north, thick woods planted on a gently rising slope form a wall that adds to the serenity of the scene. The characteristics of this planting arrangement are as follows:

1. A rich variety of plant colours with alternate appearance of typical seasonal features. In spring, there are yulan magnolias (white), Ural falsespiraeas (white), jasmines (yellow), the cherry blossom (pink) and Japanese maple (red leaves). In summer there are crapemyrtles (bright red), silk trees (pink), Chinese St. Johnswort (yellow flower) and southern magnolia (white flower). Red leaves make the major impact in autumn and the evergreen cypress adorns the winter. Various herbaceous flowers are arranged in front of the groves.

2. Proper arrangement of plants with differentiation of primary and secondary elements. A grove made up of wide-spreading trees like the umbrella-shaped silk trees planted at the highest part of the landscape naturally commands the entire scene. The big plane trees are planted on lower grounds on the opposite side so that they do not interfere with the prominence of the silk trees. In the north, the flowering hedges have comparatively straight and even canopy lines. In March when the tract of cherry blossoms in the south are in full blossom, they fit in well with the colour pattern of the vegetation.

3. Attention to the changes in the colour combinations in different seasons. In late spring and early summer, the silk trees are in full-blown red blossoms. After they shed leaves in autumn, the red-leaved trees—the Japanese maple and the trident maple—blaze out at their back, setting off the yellow-leaved plane trees on the opposite side. When the plane trees become bare, the row of evergreen cypress is revealed at their back, outlining white trunks of the plane trees. Thus, the vegetation never appears dull and withered away the whole year round.

Nevertheless, it is not necessary that every vegetation in a public garden must have

Figure 1-24 Plant matching.

a. Scarlet azaleas vs. deep-red faber maples—large-leaved herbaceous plants vs. arboreous trees.

b. Pink pineapple flowers vs. deep-red faber maples—linear-leaved herbaceous plants vs. arboreous trees.

c. Light-red Chinese flowering crabapples vs. deep-red faber maples —shrub groves vs. arboreous trees.

Figure 1-25 a   *Figure 1-25 b*

Figure 1-25 c   *Figure 1-25 d*

Figure 1-25   Examples of single-season features.

a. Woods of cherry trees in spring.

b. Woods of crapemyrtles in summer.

c. Woods of maple trees in autumn.

d. Woods of camellias in winter.

flowering plants for all the four seasons. Repetition of similar arrangements creates monotony, particularly when they appear within a limited area where too much variety will result in disorder. Usually, year-round flowerage is an asset in larger gardens only. In fact, the arrangement of plants to show seasonal features should always be based on the garden plan as a whole.

V. Ground Arrangements

For a vegetation, besides the arrangement of the major tree (or trees) and groves of other trees, the ground and the edges as well as decorative objects are also important design factors.

The usual ground treatment is to plant turf. In northern China most turf is composed of baffalo grass, *Carex callitrichos* (a kind of sedge) and Bermuda grass, whereas Japanese lawngrass and Korean velvet grass are found in the south. Turf grass in the north keeps green for over 170 days and in the south, as long as 250 days. In southern Guangdong Province, grass is green all the year round.

Besides surfacing the ground in uniform colour, the turf prevents soil erosion, keeps the air dustless and brings about favourable microclimatic changes. According to the data supplied by the municipal botanical garden of Hangzhou, the average temperature on a garden lawn is 2.3°-4°C lower than that on the city asphalt road while the relative humidity on the lawn is 2.8% higher. The green turf over a vegetation subdues the sunlight, and thereby protects the eye. However, heavy foot traffic damages lawns, so they should not be used on paths or in places where crowds gather. Instead, walks of bricks or stones can be built across or around the lawns.

The edges of a vegetation do not merely mark the borders, they are also an important part of the scenery. The plants here should be of varying heights unevenly but artistically spaced. It is not desirable to simply hedge the space with low plants. Some use groves of the evergreen flowering pineapples for edging (figure 1-27a); others use the deciduous plantain banana, which creates changes of spatial effects in winter and summer. If it is intended to create a completely secluded and tranquil space, big evergreen trees and shrubs can be thickly planted in tiers (figure 1-27b).

In a vegetation, stones or rocks are often scattered over an undulating surface and half buried in the lawn like the terminal of a mountain range in miniature. Another common decoration is shown in figure 1-28a with a picturesque column of rock standing in the center of the lawn like a gigantic vase holding the Chinese trumpet-creepers planted on top of the rock. The arrangement adds a unique feature to the scene.

In seasons when plant colours are relatively monotonous, some herbaceous flowers of various hues will enrich the colour texture. Figure 1-28b shows an artistically-arranged assembly of potted chrysanthemums of various colours to dress up an otherwise drab late autumn scene. It is also acceptable to add some decorative flowers close to the ground such as the narcissus shown in figure 1-28c.

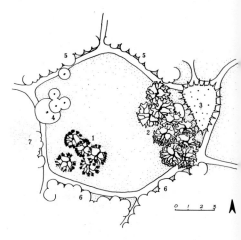

Figure 1-26 a

Figure 1-26 b

Figure 1-26 c

Figure 1-27 a

Figure 1-26 Examples of four-season features.

a. Plan: 1. Silk trees. 2. Oriental plane trees. 3. Cypresses. 4. Yulan magnolias and flowering shrubs. 5. Flowering shrubs in layers. 6. Cherry trees. 7. Trident maples.

b. The silk trees stand prominently on the highest part of the landscape.

c. In winter, the bare plane trees with white trunks stand out against the green cypresses in the background.

Figure 1-27 The functions of bordering plants.

a. Using flowering pineapple with its linear leaves as an evergreen plant for borders to match the trees in the background.

b. Using camphor trees and palms to form a green screen on the fringe.

Figure 1-27 b

Figure 1-28　Picturesque decorations for a vegetation.

a. A peculiar piece of rock on the lawn.

b. Potted chrysanthemums lacing the lawn.

c. Narcissus used to decorate a vegetation that has a wilderness aspect.

Figure 1-28 a

Figure 1-28 b

Plant Arrangements for Garden Paths

Chapter Two

Plant Arrangements for Garden Paths

The main function of a garden path is not for foot traffic but for sightseeing. The designers of Chinese garden paths have always emphasized natural twists and turns in close harmony with the scenes alongside. Therefore, the disposition of plants along garden paths should first of all point up their artistic function not only in relation to the paths themselves, but to the entire garden.

I. Characteristics of Plant Arrangements for Garden Paths

Plantings for garden paths go along with the characteristics of the paths. Some are clearly delineated, others are not (figure 2-1). However they all lead the sightseer to new scenic spots at every twist and turn. And this role is often achieved by the disposition of plants. So the plant arrangement along garden paths is usually not in monotonous rows, but determined by the artistic role intended for the paths in the overall layout of the garden. The choice of wayside trees and their arrangements should serve the same purpose. In other words, it should take into consideration the surrounding scenes such as hills, rockeries, water, conspicuous trees and others. The choice of the right kind of trees, the utilization and sometimes modification of topographic features and artistic judgement will combine to create a garden path environment which is at once colourful and functional.

Regarding the disposition of plants, the usual way of lining up the trees along the path should be replaced by naturally arranged trees, shrubs, flowers and grass. The distance between these plants and the path edges may vary, with thin and thick planting alternating. Where trees are suitable, use trees; where flowers look better, use flowers. They should be arranged in different heights and in various suitable ways.

When choosing trees, prominence should be given to one or several kinds of trees with striking characteristics. Another alternative is to use a single kind of plant in quantity to create special paths such as a path through the woods, a footpath among flowers or a pathway in a bamboo grove.

In addition, a designer of garden paths should take into consideration their multiple functions such as providing road directions and shades, marking off different areas and channelizing foot traffic. In this sense, they share some of the characteristics of the plants along the streets in cities, but they differ in certain other aspects. For instance, garden paths do not have to be shaded all the way through, for the sightseers do not necessarily walk the paths from end to end, but pause here and there or stray off at some point. This provides more flexibility for plant disposition along garden paths.

Figure 2-2 Balanced plant disposition for a garden path.

a. Plan: 1. Hedge bamboo. 2. Masson pines.

b. Sketch: A sightseer on the path. The plants on either side show balance between each other in both density and height.

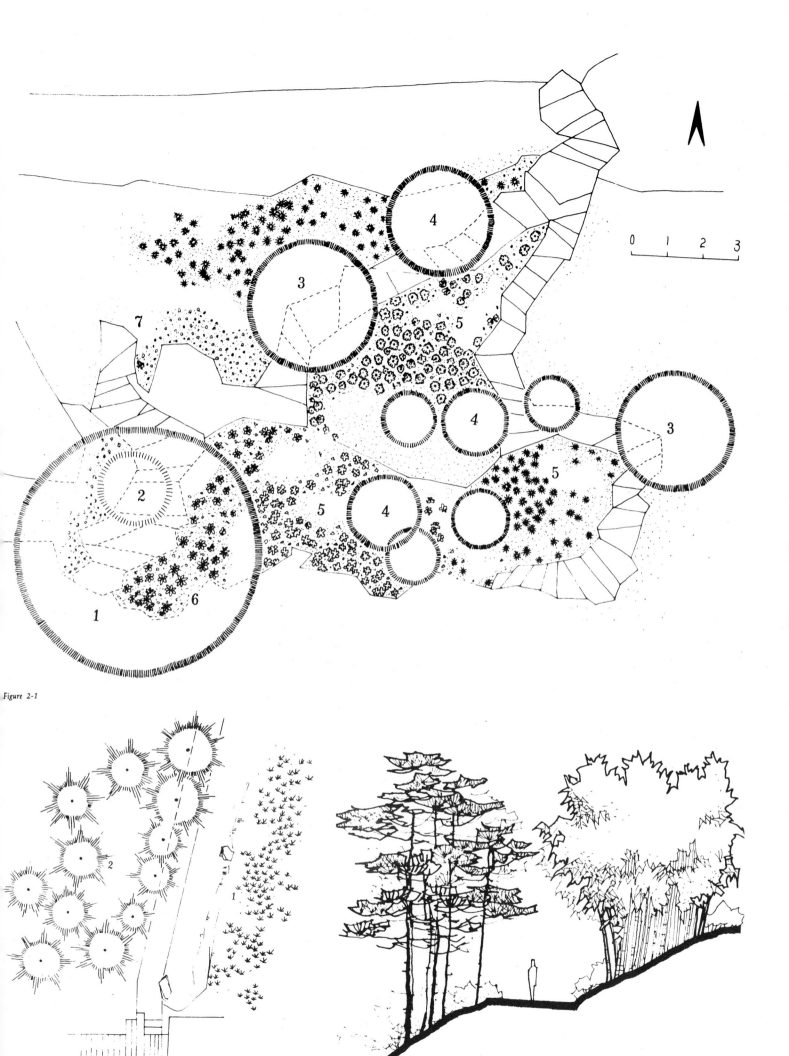

Figure 2-1

Figure 2-2 a

Figure 2-2 b

Figure 2-3   Plant disposition of a garden path in harmony with its surroundings.

a. Plan: The plants south of the path: 1. Peach (*Prunus persica var duplex*). 2. Cypress. 3. Tobira pittosporum. 4. Low flowering shrubs. The plants north of the path. 1. Peach (*Prunus persica var duplex*). 2. Glossy privet.

b. Sketch: The plant disposition in layers in the south harmonizes with the garden space in the north.

Figure 2-3 *a*

Figure 2-3 *b*

Figure 2-4—The cone-shaped deodar cedars on one side of the path and the cylinder-shaped southern magnolia on the other side form a contrast.

Figure 2-4

II. Artistic Patterns of Plant Arrangements for Garden Paths

Since the scenic value of garden paths overrides their other functions it is perhaps worthwhile to look into the general guidelines for artistic composition of plants along the paths.

1. Balance and Contrast.

When for various reasons, garden paths are not flanked by rows of plants, care should be taken to maintain balance between the vegetation on either side of the path so that it will not show abrupt twists and turns and appear detached from the rest of the scene. Figure 2-2a shows a garden path on the ridge of a hill. The path is only 2 m wide with a steep slope on one side. A tract of 8-metre-high masson pines stands on the slope, fringed by azaleas in a riot of colour. The other side of the path, which borders on a stony slope, is planted with bamboo around 3 m in height. The sparse pine trees and the dense bamboo grove, resting on grounds of different elevation (figure 2-2b) achieve a comfortable balance. The pines and the bamboo, both being evergreens, appear harmonious. Here, it would be undesirable to stress contrast by planting tall trees in high places and lower ones on low ground. Such a lopsided arrangement may cause a sense of insecurity to those walking the path.

If the landscape is flat, the plant disposition along garden paths should blend well with the surrounding environment. For instance, in the garden path plan shown in figure 2-3, the plantings on either side of the path itself are not balanced. In the south there is a screen formed by *Prunus persica var. duplex*, tobira pittosporum and cypress, and in the north only one or two groves of trees are planted for shade. But since these roadside plants are integrated with the garden further beyond in the north, they do not appear out of balance with the vegetation along the southern side of the path. The *Prunus persica* are planted at 3.5 m interval, under which azaleas and begonias are planted. On either side of the path various herbaceous flowers are grown alternately. In early spring the red and pink flowers of *Prunus persica* and cherry apple trees and the azaleas bloom in turn and form an attractive flower belt setting off the evergreen cypress. This disposition plan not only outlines the path but also takes into consideration its effect on the garden space in the north.

The element of contrast in the plant disposition for garden paths includes first of all the combination of several kinds of trees. Figure 2-4 is a main path in a park. It is 3 m wide with deodar cedars on one side and southern magnolias on the other. The cedars taper off to a point and are light green and coniferous, while the magnolias are cylindrical, dark green and broad-leaved. Despite the sharp contrasts, compositional balance is retained because they are both tall evergreen plants which combine to give a distinctive character to the scene. Another way of achieving contrast involves colour and sunlight (figure 2-5). It shows a fork of a garden path planted with Japanese maples, faber maples, osmanthus, hackberry trees and azaleas. The maples are 2.5 to 3 m in height, and scattered on the opposite side, and at the back are groves of tuftwool rhododendron. In early May, the red crowns of the maples form a pleasant contrast with white flowers of the rhododendron. In autumn, the red maples form a different contrast with the dark green leaves of the osmanthus and the Chinese hackberry. Meanwhile, because of density of trees at the intersection, the subdued light creates a contrast with the brightness in other sectors of the path, making fascinating changes of scenes.

2. The Dominant and the Subsidiary.

To obtain a clear division between the primary and the secondary, attention should be paid to the quantity and variety of trees. A garden path with trees all of the same kind gives prominence to the characteristics of this particular kind of tree in a certain season. However, for a garden path with natural appeal, a single kind of tree may appear too monotonous to give the path a rich and colourful appearance. For instance, although the trees are attractive at flowering time they may look uninteresting when the blossoms fade away. So, two or more kinds of trees are often used for a long garden road, and different trees are used for different segments. However, among these trees, one variety should dominate over others to produce a specific effect. Otherwise, it might result in disorder.

The distinction between the dominant and the subsidiary trees is not entirely marked by quantity, but more importantly by the spatial effect of their forms and colours. Sometimes, the attraction of a single large tree is stronger than that of ten smaller trees or a grove of shrubs. In addition, spatial attraction changes with time. Figure 2-6 shows a 1.5-m-wide slabstone path laid on turf. The path cuts through naturally arranged groves consisting of big, sturdy Chinese wingnuts and evergreen camphor trees, and the smaller *Prunus corasifera var. atropurpurea* of the plum family. For a time, four fast-growing Chinese wingnuts dominate this sector of the path. There is a feeling of being in a wood when walking under them. As the wingnuts get old, the camphor trees on the other side of the path will command the scene, while the six plum trees remain subsidiary throughout. Thus, the three kinds of trees each play a distinct role without creating any confusion.

In brief, the number of trees to be grown on either side of a path mainly depends on the position, character and function of the path, and the kinds of trees chosen. Along a path of medium length, it is better not to plant more than three kinds of trees and among them, one kind should stand out. Different trees can be chosen for different segments of the path.

3. Rhythm.

Some tree-lined garden paths are embellished by alternating two or more than two kinds of trees at regular intervals to create a rhythmic effect. This method is mostly applied to uniformly-built paths or those on dykes. In the scenic city of Hangzhou, for instance, there is a White Dyke in the West Lake. The traditional method of alternating one willow with one blossoming peach along the path on the dyke creates a rhythmical alternating of pink and green in spring. In figure 2-7, there is a curved path with a waterway on either side. Seasonal change in roadside vegetation is achieved by alternating groves of crapemyrtles which bear deep-red flowers in summer with groves of osmanthus with yellow flowers in autumn. However, the regular alternation of wayside trees is not suitable for a long path, for it might make the path appear uninteresting and dull, but it is often applied to scenic drives for autos or bicycles.

4. Layerage and Backgrounds.

Layered plantings along a path is mainly for embellishing and enhancing the perspective of wayside views so as to mitigate the dullness of a lengthy path. Spatial effect can be enhanced by grading the layerage from low to high away from the path. Sometimes this method is used for gradual scenic transition from the edge of the path to lawns and groves beyond. In the meantime, densely planted evergreens can serve as a screen or background. Figure 2-8 shows a 2-m-high green screen formed by densely-planted sweet viburnum with a tract of 3- to 4-m-high bamboo groves in the background. The plain layerage lends tranquility to the path.

5. The Directional Function of Garden Paths.

Wayside plants skilfully set against the surrounding scenery will guide the sightseer to ever-changing views as he ambles along the path. Thus, the disposition of wayside plants

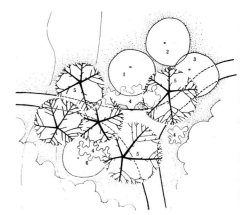

Figure 2-5

Figure 2-5   Plant disposition at a fork. Plan: 1. Osmanthus. 2. Evergreen chinkapin. 3. Hackberry. 4. Tuftwool rhododendron. 5. Japanese maple. 6. Bayberry.

Figure 2-6   Plant disposition on either side of a path with contrast between the primary and the secondary elements.

a. Plan: 1. Chinese wingnut. 2. Camphor tree. 3. Purple-leaved plum. Trees on the left are the primary element; those on the right are secondary. The arrangement is in harmony with the curves of the path.

b. View of the Chinese wingnuts and the camphor trees on the left side of the path.

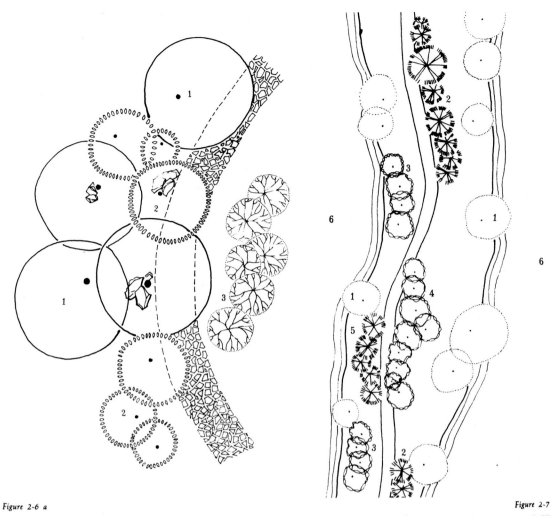

Figure 2-6 a

Figure 2-7   A garden path with groves of different trees alternately planted on either side. Trees shown in the plan: 1. Footcatkin willows. 2. Osmanthus. 3. Camphor trees. 4. Crapemyrtles. 5. Camellias. 6. Water surface.

Figure 2-7

Figure 2-6 b

Figure 2-8   Densely planted sweet viburnums with bamboo groves as background form a green screen.

Figure 2-8

Figure 2-9

Figure 2-9   Catalpas lining the garden
path leading to a pagoda.

Figure 2-10   The wayside camphor tree
provides both visual enjoyment and
landmark.

Figure 2-10

Figure 2-11   The foliage forms a
"picture frame" at the end of a hill path.
In the distance, a river, a village and the
fields virtually become part of the
garden view.

Figure 2-12   A heavily-shaded path
winding over hills.

a. Plan: 1. Camphor trees. 2. Glossy
privets and other trees. 3. Porch. 4. Pool
5. Masson pines and *Cyclobalanopsis
glauca* of the oak family. 6. Bamboo
groves. 7. Small bamboo garden.

b. An ascending narrow path lined with
tall trees gives the effect of a mountain
forest.

Figure 2-11

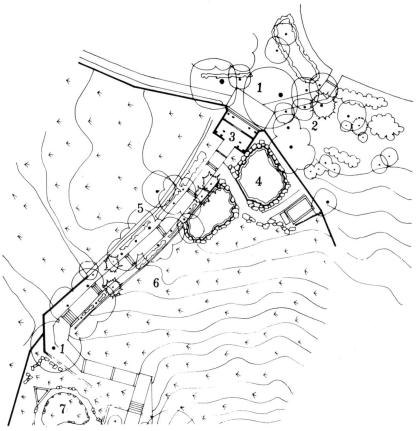

Figure 2-12 a

Figure 2-12 b

is often one of the criteria for judging the ability of the designer.

In most cases, a guiding path leads to a conspicuous object lying straight ahead, such as a building, a statue, a rockery or a picturesque plant. A path of this type is usually lined with neat rows of trees on either side, showing the object in the distance in natural perspective. Figure 2-9 is a straight path 4 m in width and 50 m in length, leading to a pagoda. Planted on each side are catalpa trees in single file with sparse branches and leaves. The moderately upward slope enhances the perspective, with the partially revealed pagoda ahead towering above the foliage. The broad leaves of the catalpa provide an interesting contrast with the spiral-shaped top of the pagoda.

Sometimes, a particularly interesting tree or a grove of such trees at the side of a path can serve as objects for enjoyment and a landmark as well. In figure 2-10, the oriental sweetgum along a garden path in a city is a sight for enjoyment in autumn. When a precious tree is in the way of a garden path, the tree should be protected and made part of the wayside scene.

Another approach to design is to make good use of other natural features such as curves of the terrain, the shape of trees and the height and width of their crowns. Figure 2-11 is a path on the slope of a hill. The crowns of the oriental sweetgums on both sides of the path meet to form a leafy frame through which to view the river scenery in the distance. The sightseer would feel as though he were looking at a framed picture. However, the trees used to produce the "picture frame" against the scenery in the background must have beautiful trunks, a dense canopy and a high branch point, such as Chinese soapberry, Chinese scholar tree, Chinese sopium, camphor tree, silk tree, elm tree and masson pine.

III. Plantings for Special Garden Paths

Some paths in Chinese gardens bear distinctive characteristics accentuated by special planting schemes.

1. Hill Paths.

Chinese gardens stress naturalness. They can often produce a small natural environment within a limited area, which is aptly described by a Chinese saying: See Nature in miniature. A city garden often has a limited area on flat grounds. But it is possible to build a path bearing some semblance of a country scene through gardening and planting.

Figure 2-12 is a curved path on a slope with towering trees irregularly planted on both sides. They include the masson pine, the camphor tree and the *Cyclobalanopsis glauca* of the oak family, whose spreading foliage keeps the entire path under shade. The trees are about 20 m in height and the path is 3 m wide. The dense woods plus the bamboo groves beside the trees create an enjoyable environment. In addition, the path on a 10° to 20° slope gradually winds upward, increasing the depth of perspective at different levels. A murmuring stream cutting across the bamboos adds tranquility and country charm.

Even on flat ground, a sense of being in the woods can be achieved through plantings and slight transformation of the topography. Figure 2-13 is a winding path 1.5 m in width. The path surface is lowered and the height of the slopes is raised on both sides by about 2 m slightly above eye level. Tall leafy trees such as oriental sweetgums, sawtooth oaks, Chinese hackberry trees and black locusts are planted 0.3 to 1.5 m away from the edge of the path at between 0.5 to 4 m intervals to keep the path completely under shade. The winding course and its sunken surface creates the environment of a small path amid thick woods.

No matter whether a natural hill path or an artificial garden path, the charm of a wooded space depends on the following elements:

(1) The wayside trees should be tall and straight, keeping the ratio of 6:1 up to 10:1 between the height of the trees and the width of the path. Arboreous trees are preferred. The ground vegetation underneath the trees should be low plants (use shrubs sparingly) so as to stress the contrast between the height of the trees and the narrowness of the path, which is typical of mountain paths.

(2) The trees on either side of the path should be densely planted so as to produce a heavily shaded environment like in a mountain forest.

(3) The trees should be in layers thick enough to limit the depth of vision with their foliage and simulate a path amid a forest.

(4) The path should be in a garden with undulating slopes. The steeper the slope, the stronger the likeness to a mountain path. If the slope is not steep enough, it can be emphasized by lowering the path surface thereby making the slope nearby higher, or by planting tall trees on the slope so that the sightseer sees at his level of vision only groves of trees, which adds to the feeling of strolling in a mountain forest.

(5) The garden path should be long and curved. The length adds depth and the curves add serenity.

(6) The designer of a garden path should make full use of the natural valleys, streams, crags, groves, etc. so as to stress the atmosphere of a natural mountain forest.

2. Bamboo Path.

Chinese bamboo in more than 200 varieties is grown mostly south of 35° N. latitude. They are commonly found in natural scenic spots or in gardens. Bamboo is evergreen and graceful, particularly the leaves. The tallest ones such as the furry bamboo can reach 30 m while the shortest variety, the broadleaf sasa, is only about 20 cm. Morphologically speaking, bamboo plants are either scattered or in groves or mixed with other plants. Bamboo is used in gardens for many purposes, such as forming a forest, lining a path or a stream, embellishing a slope or a section of a garden, fencing a flower bed or building, a veranda or pavilion. The bamboo paths especially have many distinctive characteristics.

Besides being evergreen, bamboo adds tranquility to the environment. When planted along a path, it produces varied effects on the design of the garden. Figure 2-14a is a completely closed-in space along a curved, bamboo path. The low walls separating the bamboo from the path accentuates the tranquility of the space. In figure 2-14b, in a comparatively open space, some densely planted bamboos round the corner of the path creates the atmosphere of "being deep in a bamboo forest." The common types of bamboo paths in gardens are as follows:

(1) A small path in a bamboo grove.

This is the most common type of bamboo path in a garden. The path is either lined with bamboo on either side or cuts across a bamboo grove. In either way, a tranquil environment results. Figure 2-15 is a hill path 13 m long, with bamboos on both sides. A plum tree bending over the first few steps of the path marks the beginning of the hill climb. A grove of bamboos to the right of the plum tree are an added attraction. The bending bamboo tops on either side intermesh to form a canopy over the path. The osmanthus tree in the midst of the bamboo smells sweet in autumn, and the cherry tree in the grove graces the path with its flowerage in spring. They enhance the artistic appeal of a small path in a bamboo grove.

(2) A curved bamboo path.

A path of this type is often characterized by its fascinating tranquility. There is such a path in Hangzhou. It is 53.3 m long and 1.5 m wide, leading to buildings on either end (figure 2-16). Planted on both sides are fine bamboos, the tonkin cane and the henon bamboo about 2 m in height. The path extends on the bank of a pond planted with

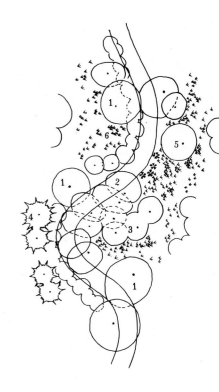

Figure 2-13 a

Figure 2-13   A curved path deep in a forest.

a. Plane: 1. Oriental sweetgums. 2. Sawtooth oaks. 3. *Cyclobalanopsis glauca*. 4. Masson pines. 5. Hackberries. 6. Bamboo grove.

b. Sketch: A curved path across a large slope is without steps to make it appear natural. A strong feeling of seclusion is provided by the thick foliage.

Figure 2-14   Two different ways of building a bamboo path.

a. In closed-in style, a curved path has bamboo foliage overhead and is lined by walls. One only sees bamboo while walking on the path.

b. In open style, the path leads the sightseer to other scenic spots before it reaches the bamboo grove at the end of the path.

Figure 2-13 b

Figure 2-14 a

Figure 2-15

62

Figure 2-15   Sketch: A completely
closed-in bamboo path.

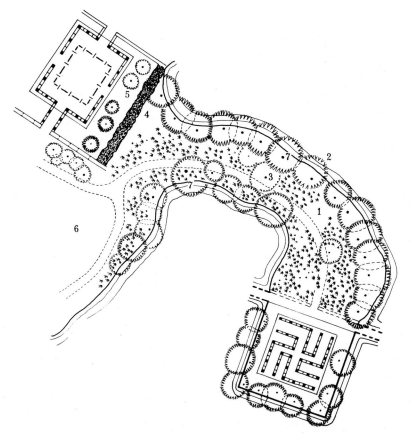

Figure 2-16 a

Figure 2-16   A bamboo path leading to
a tranquil setting.

a. Plan: Buildings are on two ends and
water on both sides. Grown along the
path are: 1. Henon bamboo. 2.
Footcatkin willow. 3. Tallow tree
(Sapium sebiferum). 4. Grove of sweet
viburnum. 5. Crapemyrtle. 6. Lawn. 7.
Java bishopwood.

b. A section of the bamboo path.

Figure 2-16 b

63

Figure 2-17 A bamboo path deep in the mountain.

a. The path is 4 m in width, running through a grove of 20-m-high bamboo.

b. Sketch: A 4-m-high wayside pavilion housing a tablet and 35-m-high oriental sweetgums towering over the pavilion form a strong contrast and a scenic accent.

Figure 2-17 b

Figure 2-18 a

Figure 2-18 b

Figure 2-18   A flower path.
a. A path in the midst of cherry trees.
b. A path lined with crapemyrtles.

footcatkin willow, and Java bishopwood. The bamboo grove is mixed with some colourful tallow trees. The low but thick bamboo grove keeps the pond almost out of sight so that the path appears closed-in and tranquil. The path, though fairly straight for the most part, bends sharply toward either end. So the sightseer starting from one end cannot see the other end until he reaches there. At one end of the path is a hedge of sweet viburnum which enhances the seclusiveness of the spot. Coming out from the bend of the path, the sightseer finds himself on a small open lawn. The abrupt change of scenery reminds one of a familiar verse by an ancient Chinese poet:

> *Suddenly before your eyes, there appears*
> *A refreshing scene of dense willows and bright flowers.*

Here the proper handling of lighting and curvature is of great importance. Subdued light accentuates tranquility whereas "brightness" fulfils the sightseers' hunt for fascinating scenery. The curved path described here illustrates this gardening technique. The bamboos should be densely planted and taller than man. Sometimes one or two tall broad-leaved trees mixed with the bamboos can offer better shade and further darken the area so that the field of vision is completely confined within the space of the path.

(3) A bamboo path deep in a mountain.

Figure 2-17 shows such a path in south China. 800 m long and 4 m wide, the path winds through a dense forest of furry bamboo which averages 20 m in height. A pavilion stands at the starting point, with a trident maple by its side as a landmark. About 300 steps further, there is another pavilion where one hears a murmuring stream in the bamboo grove. Further on about 150 steps, a third pavilion sits right across the path for the sightseer to take a rest and enjoy the shadows of the bamboo leaves through latticed windows. Another 100 steps takes one to three large oriental sweetgums over 35 m in height and 4.5 m in circumference. Under the trees, there is a 4-metre-high pavilion housing a tablet. Dwarfed by the towering trees around, the tablet is an added interest to the rustic beauty of the bamboo grove. Finally, 150 steps further, comes the end of the path—an ancient temple, around which fountains trickle amid thickets of green bamboo and many towering trees. Here the sightseer can relish the beauty of nature in the seclusion of forested mountains.

The mountain path described above demonstrates that for those bamboo paths that are several hundred metres in length, it is preferable to make use of varied elements such as water, rockery, buildings and large trees to enrich the settings and produce an artistic environment. High trees can create feelings of darkness and coolness, or mark the turns or segments of a path. Natural or man-made bends of a stream, a placid pond, a whispering streamlet or a small crystal-clear water surface adds tranquility to the environment. Well-designed pavilions, corridors, gateways, bridges and wayside benches not only provide a place for rest, but also bring out a contrast between natural beauty and the geometric shapes of man-made works. Stone carvings, latticed windows or literary couplets depicting bamboo in artistic forms will add a human dimension to natural scenery.

3. Flower Path.

Flower paths are a special attraction in gardens. They produce an environment of colours with their varied blooms or beautiful leaves, bearing distinctive seasonal characteristics. Particularly during the flowering periods, the attraction is compelling.

The following are flower paths often found in Chinese gardens.

Cherry flower path. Cherry trees have spreading branches, and when in full bloom, they are resplendent with light pink flowers. Figure 2-18a shows a 3-m-wide road lined with cherry trees on one side and bright-coloured saucer magnolia on the other. Accompanying the cherry trees are evergreen palms to fill in the spaces between the cherries. The turf on the roadside sown with creeping oxalis adds to the attraction of the path.

Crapemyrtle path. The crapemyrtles' twisting yellowish-white stems and branches and their showy pink, white flowers lasting as long as three months (from June to August) make them one of the favourite plantings for wayside decoration (figure 2-18b).

Osmanthus path. Although the shape and colour of the sweet osmanthus are not very striking, its flowering period lasts over one month in the fall. This, together with its intoxicating fragrance, makes it a unique roadside attraction in autumn when flowers are relatively few.

Plum path. Few trees bloom in winter. However, the plum trees flower even in heavy snow. The plum blossoms are yellow and emit a clinging fragrance. Plum trees are shrubs but have long and thin branches. When thickly planted along a path, a sweet fragrance will permeate the path from end to end.

In brief, to build an attractive flower path, the first thing is to choose the right kind of plants. They should have large, showy flowers and beautiful shapes, and are striking in colour. It is preferable to have trees that first produce flowers and then leaves. Those that have long flowering periods and pleasant fragrance are also good choices. The trees, especially the shrubs, should be densely planted. They are always planted several lines deep and never in a single line. Besides the flowering trees, there should be some evergreen trees or shrubs in the background or as subsidiary plants so as to strengthen the colour contrast and compactness of the wayside scene.

Paths with fall tints formed by the colour leaves in autumn can often be scenic attractions in gardens. For example, the yellow leaves of Chinese soapberry (figure 2-19) and the red leaves of the oriental sweetgum last as long as one month. These plants can make a whole path glow with warm colours.

Figure 2-20   Paths.

a. Steps on a slope with shrubs and rocks alongside enhance rustic charm.

b. A round·flat path with red flowers grown on the terrace on the right side and white ones on the ground on the left side. They are of the same height.

c. A path winding over an open flat ground with a few trees and shrubs, suggesting spaciousness.
d. A path in a small garden. This kind of path can be made to look natural and attractive with various plant arrangements. It should be mosaically paved.

Figure 2-19   A path graced by the yellow leaves of Chinese soapberries.

Figure 2-19

Figure 2-20 a

Figure 2-20 b

Figure 2-20 c

Figure 2-20 d

4. Small Paths.

Like veins in human body, small garden paths spread in different lengths and directions, but are mostly about one m in width. Plantings for these paths focus mainly on their scenic value.

The opening of a path in a wood often produces a closed space with dense shade. Among man-made gardens with rockeries or in natural mountain woods, there are often narrow, stepped slopes with climbing plants such as the Chinese star jasmine and the creeping fig-tree. They add interest to the path (figure 2-20a). Although some paths are paved in geometric designs, they are not necessarily matched by balanced plantings. Figure 2-20b is a curved path. There is a flower bed on a raised platform on one side planted with scarlet sage, and the other side is a low green hedgerow of boxwood, along which are a densely-planted row of flowering pineapples. The plant disposition on either side is not symmetrical, but it forms a colour contrast between red and white, and presents a balance in height between the flower bed and the hedgerow.

When building a path in an open vegetation, one or two large trees or some groves of flowering shrubs planted alongside the path will create a bright and spacious setting (figure 2-20c).

A garden path of the natural type is often found in sophisticated garden settings. Rocks are placed at random along the path. Sometimes, rocks and dwarf lilyturf are scattered on the lawn on either side. The trees along the path differ in height; some are in their natural shape and some are pruned. They are planted at irregular intervals. Most of the paths are mosaically paved without shades and offer a good field of vision (figure 2-20d).

Figure 2-21

IV. Plantings for Component Parts of a Garden Path.

Although plantings for the component parts of a garden path do not play a prominent role in the whole design, they deserve careful consideration, nevertheless.

1. Path Borders.

Vegetation at the edges embodies the low flowering plants, hedges and lawns immediately alongside the paths. Sometimes, it also includes trees and shrubs grown next to the edging. Plant disposition for this part of the path should serve to identify, embellish and enhance the guiding function of the path. For example, the use of hedges can help direct the sightseer's line of vision to the specific scenery ahead. And the right use of trees and shrubs can make the path appear more secluded and longer. When the wayside plants are spaced irregularly and the space between the plants and the edging is varied, the path will appear more natural than otherwise. Under certain circumstances, wayside plants play the role of separating one garden zone from another.

(1) Grass edging.

One feature of Chinese gardens is the growing of dwarf lilyturf at path edges. This is especially popular in areas along the Changjiang (Yangtse) River. Dwarf lilyturf is evergreen, proliferous and free from diseases of pests. Besides its decorative role, it enriches the wayside scene and prevents soil erosion when there are slopes on both sides of a path (figure 2-21).

(2) Flower borders. The beauty of a garden path can be greatly enhanced by growing annual or perennial herbaceous flowers on its edges, which will look like colour belts in a green garden setting. Figure 2-22a shows the white-flowered autumn zephyrlily on the edges of a path with blooming osmanthus on both sides and a grove of scarlet sage ahead. The path is a happy combination of colour, fragrance and scenic beauty. Some paths have low walls on both sides to keep away dust. It is then desirable to plant flowering shrubs that have weeping branches like the jasmine to hang over the walls so as to increase the layerage of the wayside vegetation (figure 2-22b).

(3) Hedges.

Hedges are a common feature along city streets and garden paths. The heights of hedges vary from 0.5 m to 3 m but average about 1.2 m. They separate a path from its surroundings besides producing the aesthetic effects of a green or a colour belt.

There are no fixed rules for the ratio between the height of a hedge and the width of a garden path. It mainly depends on the designer's intention. High hedges along a narrow path will make it appear narrower and longer. However, this method is often used in walled-in gardens, and seldom in open garden space. If a broad field of vision is desired to enjoy the scenery surrounding the path, the hedges should not be too high. Figure 2-23a shows a 2-m-wide row proportionally matched with a 0.8-m-high hedgerow. As for the thickness of the hedges, two or three layers are usually needed, with the plants arranged at staggered intervals.

For hedges it is preferable to choose slow-growing evergreens to facilitate pruning. In north China, the plants commonly chosen for hedges are oriental arborvitae, Chinese juniper (figure 2-23b), and boxwood. Some deciduous plants are also used, such as Siberian elm, Chinese hawthorn, fortune fontanesia and maple. In the south, the commonly used plants include evergreens such as the Chinese littleleaf box tree, glossy privet, tobira pittosporum and augustine rhododendron. In gardens, flowering shrubs are used to make "flower

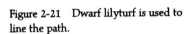

Figure 2-21 Dwarf lilyturf is used to line the path.

Figure 2-22 a

Figure 2-22 b

Figure 2-22   Flowering plants to
decorate path borders.

a. White autumn zephyrlily along the
borders sets off the scarlet sage ahead.

b. Overhanging yellow winter jasmine
breaks the harsh lines of the walls
protecting the slope.

hedges," which are usually composed of a single kind or two kinds of alternately planted flower plants. It is best to choose varieties which have long flowering periods and bear dense flowers, such as the seven-sisters Japanese rose.

2. Paving Decoration.

Planting the surface of a garden path does not mean the growing of plants on the path surface. One way to dress up a path in a Chinese garden is to plant grass on the borders between the slabs of stone or cement bricks that are set in various patterns on the turf to form a walkway (figure 2-24). The paved surface, besides serving as a distinctive decorative mark of the path, also lowers the surface temperature. It has been found that at 10 cm above ground, the temperature over pavements with inlaid grass is 2°C lower than that without grass.

Paths that are traversed by very few people are occasionally turfed and bordered by low herbaceous flowers. These flowers are here and there allowed to vegetate onto the path itself, which creates naturalness and adds a softer texture (figure 2-25).

In one Chinese garden, there is a "plum shadow" path. A single plum tree stands by its side and throws on the pavement a shadow which is traced by inlaid cobble stones. Once a day, when the right hour arrives, the real shadow falls in with the inlaid image on the ground, offering an added attraction to the sightseers (figure 2-26).

3. Intersections.

The plant disposition at intersections involves settings at the four corners or the centre of a crossroads, the corners of a fork, or the terminals of a path. The arrangements vary with the characteristics, widths and lengths of the paths, and the functional and aesthetic purposes they serve.

It is generally inadvisable to grow trees or shrubs near intersections that may impair the line of vision. What is preferable is to plant low shrubs or large trees which have over 1.5-m-high branch points. Under certain circumstances, rocks can be put at random at the intersections together with flowers and grass or with low and pruned plants.

The plant disposition at a fork mainly serves a marking and guiding purpose. Figure 2-27 shows the scenes at a fork. Some 20 3-m-high weeping yellow forsythias are lined against a backdrop of 20-m-tall dark green deodar cedars. The difference in colour and height, and the contrast between bending branches and straight trunks effectively decorate and mark the fork. Another fork is situated near the lawn at the entrance of a public garden with plenty of open space around (figure 2-28). Planted at the intersection are tracts of tobira pittosporum and Japanese rose which flower from May to July, decorating the edges of the lawn and marking the direction of the paths. On the lawns beyond are layers of vegetation consisting of roses (0.35 m in height), tobira pittosporum (1.5 m), crapemyrtles (2-3 m) and Chinese juniper (4-5 m). The layer arrangement makes a gradual transition from the lawn to the groves (figure 2-28).

The scenes at either end of a garden path often consist of a combination of plants and such garden features as rockeries, flower beds or buildings. If only plants are used, the choice of trees must be made very carefully so as to make the plantings stand out. For example, at the entrance of a public garden, there is an extended vegetation screen made up of faber maple and other colour-leaved trees mixed with large groves of deodar cedars. Some rockeries stand in the foreground (figure 2-29). Some path entrances are graced by artfully designed combinations of rockery and special plants like the broad-leaved herbaceous alocasia and dwarf lilyturf.

Flowering shrubs like the Chinese redbud, when grown round the bend of a garden path, will function as a landmark and draw the interest of the sightseer to go further on (figure 2-30), especially when they sway gently in a breeze.

Figure 2-23 a

Figure 2-23 Hedges.

a. A hedge of Chinese little leaf box.

b. A hedge of Chinese juniper.

Figure 2-24 In-laid decorations on cement pavements.

a. Cracked-ice design.

b. Oblique checkered design.

c. Herringbone design.

Figure 2-24 a

Figure 2-24 b

Figure 2-24 c

Figure 2-25   Decorations on a turfed path.
Small flowering shrubs grown at the borders with branches randomly bending toward the path make it look natural.

Figure 2-26   A special decorative feature. The shadow of a plum tree coincides with the design on the pavement once on each clear day.

Figure 2-27   Contrasting scenes of towering evergreen cedars and the golden weeping forsythia at the entrance of a path.

Figure 2-25

Figure 2-26

Figure 2-28

Figure 2-28 Plant disposition at a road fork. Contrast is provided by round-shaped tobira pittosporum and tower-shaped Chinese juniper. The other two corners are decorated with Japanese rose which helps to indicate road directions.

Figure 2-29

Figure 2-29 An attractive and colourful combination of planting and rockeries at the entrance of a public garden.

Figure 2-30 The single Chinese redbud around the corner of a curved path serves well as a landmark.

Figure 2-30

Plant Arrangements for Water Gardening

Chapter Three

Plant Arrangements for Water Gardening

Water scenery is found in most man-made or natural gardens. The scenes vary in a thousand and one ways, depending on the natural conditions and the intention of the designers. Some planners exploit the grandeur of rivers, lakes, sea views or waterfalls; others use ponds, water courses or streamlets to add tranquility. Some of these water features are static, others dynamic. Some are suitable for boating, swimming or skating, other as tiny as one square metre specially designed to raise fish for enjoyment. Water can produce different sounds. A brook murmurs; water trickling down on a well tinkles; a waterfall roars. All this adds interest to gardens. Some people rightly say that "water is the soul of a garden." However, whether the water constitutes the major scene, or plays a supplementary role, or is just a point of interest, it needs the embellishment of plants.

I. Plantings for Different Waterscapes

Lakes: Lakes are the most common water scenery in Chinese gardens and scenic spots. There are as many as 36 lakes that have been named as "West Lake." Among them the one in Hangzhou is the most famous. It covers an area of 5.2 km² and abounds in wonderful scenes (figure 3-1). Besides the striking beauty of the lake and the hills on its shores, the seasonal changes in the shapes and colours of the plants along the banks impart special charm and liveliness to the surrounding landscape. The willow- and peach-tree-lined Bai Causeway in the north of the lake is typical of the traditional plant disposition around West Lake. The oriental plane trees along the northern bank, the fallow trees on the Sunset Hill in the south and the groves of metasequoias on the west bank form a well-known autumn feature of West Lake with their red and yellow leaves.

Ponds: Plant disposition around ponds gives scope for the creativity of the garden designer. For instance, to stress spring scenery, azaleas are grown by the pond (figure 3-2). In March the scarlet flowers offset the evergreen trees in the background, casting shadows in the water and providing a wonderful spring accent. Figure 3-3 shows a pond in a botanical garden. The plants are arranged not only to meet the needs of scientific study but also in careful consideration of seasonal features. Rockeries on the bank are embellished by dwarf lilyturf and colourful flowering shrubs. In the pond are water-lilies and some other aquatic plants. Besides a pavilion, the pond is surrounded by trees, shrubs and turf. They include cherry trees, thumberg spiraea, faber maple, oriental sweetgum, metasequoia, China cypress and bold cypress. Together, they form charming tapestries of spring and autumn foliage.

Figure 3-4 shows a natural pond. The vegetation here is mainly composed of large evergreen camphor trees, *Phoebe sheareri* and turf. Although there are no flowers or man-made rockeries around, the clear and tranquil pond presents an aura of serenity.

Figure 3-1 Figure 3-2

Figure 3-1 A bird's eye view of West
Lake in Hangzhou. The water area is 5.2
km². It is a famous scenic spot in China.

Figure 3-2 Springtime at a pond seen
through the images of green trees and
red flowers reflected in water.

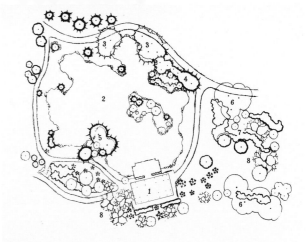

Figure 3-3 a

Figure 3-3 b

Figure 3-3 c

Figure 3-3 A natural pond in a botanical garden.

a. Plan: 1. Waterside pavilion. 2. Pond. 3. Metasequoias. 4. Baldcypresses. 5. Masson pines. 6. Oriental sweetgums. 7. Thunberg spiraea. 8. Cherry trees.

b. Spring scenery around a pond.

c. Autumn scenery around a pond.

Figure 3-4

Figure 3-4 A simple, tranquil pond.

Figure 3-5

Figure 3-5 A fish pond where trees should be planted sparsely.

Figure 3-6

Figure 3-7

Figure 3-7   A stream in a valley. The trees along the stream and the stepping stones and headstones in the water are carefully arranged to create sounds and scenes in a rustic setting.

Figure 3-6   Sketch: A fountain. The water area should not be too large and the plant disposition too elaborate to keep the natural beauty.

Sometimes, to create a heavily-shaded water surface in the woods, hygrophilous herbaceous plants such as the day-lilies are grown underneath large trees which are thickly planted around the pond. The water surface, obscured by the shadows of the trees, creates a unique garden environment.

Springs. In Chinese gardens, springs are usually square-shaped in which goldfish are raised. These fish ponds should blend well with the pattern of neighbouring buildings, and invoke special interests. Figure 3-5 shows such a fish pond. There aren't many plants around so as to make it easier for people to watch the fish and also to allow more sunlight to come through, a factor to be taken into consideration when making the design.

In figure 3-6, the fountain at the crossroads only has an area of 1 m² and is less than 1 m² deep. There are two carved Chinese characters *"yin quan"* (seal fountain) on the stone wall overlooking the fountain in the north. (Chinese ancient events were often carved on metal or stone in the way seals are carved.—*Translator's note.*) The inscription implies that scholars often come here to study ancient epigraphy. Stones are laid along the banks of the little pond and mixed with bushes of dwarf lilyturf. The evergreen bamboo groves on the west side help to create a plain and quiet environment for the literati.

Streams in valleys. A stream in a valley provides a natural scenery characterized by depth and shadiness. Plant disposition in this case should take these characteristics into consideration. The "Jiu Xi Shiba Jian" (nine streamlets and eighteen gullies) in Hangzhou is one such example. The stream in 9 segments twists along a path (now a motorway) for about 6 km with hills on both sides. Planted on the hilltops are oriental sweetgums, camphor trees and masson pines. The lower slopes are verdant tea farms. Water plants grow in abundance on the banks of the water course. Stepping stones are placed in the stream, and when walking on them, one feels as if the stones were moving in the running water. At places where there is a drop, headstones laid in the cascade produce musical gurgles. Here the landscape and the colours and sounds combine to produce a superb natural scenery of streams and valleys (figure 3-7). Another stream 60 m long and 1 m wide traverses a flat terrain. The plantings consist of cherry trees, yulan magnolias, azaleas and cherry apple trees scattered along the turfed banks embellished by rockeries. The stream comes out from the groves. In springtime, flowers bloom in many layers in a riot of colour, which earns the watercourse the poetic name of "flower stream" (figure 3-8).

Branch streams. Vegetation for branch streams in Chinese gardens generally consists of a single kind of tree to create a distinctive effect. Figures 3-9 a and b present two branch streams in different garden settings. One is lined with *Salix magnifica* which produces shade in summer and the other, with cottonrose hibiscus which blooms in luxuriance in autumn. Whatever plants are chosen, it is always preferable to grow them close to the banks to enhance the atmosphere of seclusion and tranquility.

II. Waterside Plantings

One decisive factor in forming a waterside vegetation is putting plants very close to the water, and the plants should be moisture tolerant.

It is particularly important to choose the right kind of trees to form the major element of waterside scenery. Since the water surface is often open and broad, the line of vision is easily diverted. The scenic composition can gain by giving prominence to major plant groves. The shapes and sizes of the major plants at the waterside should match the dimension of the water surface. For large rivers and lakes or on seasides, it is preferable to use large trees such as camphor trees, banyan trees and king-size coconut trees to form the

Figure 3-9 a

Figure 3-10 a

Figure 3-9 b

Figure 3-10 b

Figure 3-9   Branch stream.

a. A stream lined with footcatkin willows to provide shade in summer.

b. A stream lined with cottonrose hibiscus which flowers in autumn.

Figure 3-8   A "flower stream."

Figure 3-10   Matching the trees and the water surface.

a. Large plants such as the camphor trees are grown by the side of extended water surface to create balance.

b. Medium-sized trees match well with a smaller water surface and the exotic stone bridge.

major scene (figure 3-10a). For small and medium-sized bodies of water, smaller trees or shrubs are preferable (figure 3-10b).

Plant disposition by the waterside should take into consideration the colours of the trunks, leaves, flowers and fruits, which should match the water scene. Since the water surface is usually greenish, the leaf colours of the major plants should be light green, deep green or dark green so as to complement the water shade. For instance, in figure 3-11a the trees are mainly the red-leaved faber maple accompanied by dark green southern magnolias and light green reeds, pointing up a colour contrast between red and different shades of green. The colours stand out against, and yet blend well with, the green water. Sometimes, a grove of colourful shrubs, such as azalea in full bloom by the waterside adds a seasonal feature (figure 3-11b). In another instance, a single 30-year-old wistaria by the side of a water area presents a delicate and tranquil atmosphere through contrast with the background of thick, bright green vegetation (figure 3-11c). A large tract of the same kind of tree such as the metasequoia at the waterside produces a remarkably artistic effect (figure 3-12).

Tall plants in groups near the water can create a vertical "green screen" as a background for other waterside plants and various garden features to enhance the verdancy of the water scene. Figure 3-13a shows a 30-m-high "green screen" by a pond 15 m in width. The "screen" is made up of a rich variety of natural mountain trees. The white buildings beside the pond accentuate the height of the tree-mantled hillsides. Climbing plants grow in abundance in the woods. Sitting by the pond and listening to the birds gives one the feeling of being in a mountain forest, tranquil and secluded. When the water surface is small with no hills around, an artificial "green screen" can be created by building walls around the pond and covering them with climbing plants such as the creeping fig-tree and the Japanese creeper. Some flowering shrubs like the cottonrose hibiscus can be grown in front of the "green screen," adding colour to the water scenery (figure 3-13b). The use of "green screen" is especially suitable for ponds which are surrounded by a great variety of flowers or are elaborately decorated on the banks. A uniform "green screen" helps to blend the details into a plain, unitary scene.

In water gardening, low, water-tolerant herbaceous plants are often grown intermittently on the banks. In autumn and winter, potted cold-resistant herbaceous plants such as feverfew chrysanthemum can be placed among the rockeries on the bank. In southern China where it is warm and damp, bushes of dwarf lilyturf are frequently matched with lakeside rockeries (figure 3-14). The grass also serves to protect the banks against erosion.

III. Plantings on Water Surfaces

Water surfaces are an important element in enlarging the garden space and increasing its attractiveness. Using water surface as basic colour and embellishing it with a good variety of water plants extends the garden's vegetation area and provides an interesting contrast between the water plants and the plants on the bank.

Large areas of aquatic plants are both attractive and profitable. In Beijing's Summer Palace, large sectors of the lake are planted to waterlilies, and in June and July, their mild fragrance wafted on the breeze is a captivating summertime feature (figure 3-15).

The water plants should match with the surroundings. Generally speaking, it is not advisable to cover a whole pond with them. A certain part of the water surface should be left open, especially for producing shadows of the vegetation on the bank (figure 3-16). Water plants of special appeal should be grown at spots frequently visited by people. For example, figure 3-17 shows a precious species of waterlilies by the side of an ancient pavilion

Figure 3-11 a

Figure 3-11   Colour scheme of the trees at the waterside.

a. Faber maples, southern magnolia and reeds positioned against water present colour contrasts between red, white and green.

b. A spring scenery with red flowers in green foliage.

c. White wistarias set against green groundcovers and water.

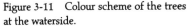

Figure 3-11 c

housing a tablet, where visitors must pass by. After seeing the carvings on the tablet, they naturally turn to relish the water lilies in the adjacent pond.

Figure 3-11 b

Figure 3-12

Figure 3-12
A single kind of tree grown in quantity along a large body of water presents a distinctive view when scanned from a distance.

Figure 3-13 a

Figure 3-13 b

Figure 3-13 Sketch: Vertical green backgrounds.

a. A green mountainside overlooking a pond.

b. A green screen formed by espaliers grown on a wall.

Figure 3-14 a

Figure 3-14 b

Figure 3-14 c

Figure 3-14 Waterside plant disposition.

a. Groves of reeds.

b. Groves of tricolour viola and feverfew chrysanthemum.

c. Dwarf lilyturf and rocks.

Figure 3-15   Waterlilies in Kunming Lake in the Summer Palace, Beijing.

Figure 3-16   When growing water plants, a certain amount of space should be left on the water surface for the reflections of the plants on the bank.

Figure 3-17   Precious pygmy waterlilies grown in the water near an ancient memorial pavilion enhance the beauty of both the aquatic plants and the pavilion.

Figure 3-15   *Figure 3-16*

IV. Artistic Composition of Water Plants

The plant disposition in ancient Chinese gardens centred around the plants' shapes and their ecological characteristics. The Chinese poet Lu You (1125-1210) described lakeside weeping willows with the following verse:

Willows in early spring breeze
Swaying and beckoning at me.

In an ancient Chinese classics "On Vegetation", the weeping willow was described as something that should be grown by the side of ponds, with its drooping branches gracefully brushing the surface of the water. It has thus become a tradition in Chinese gardens to grow weeping willows by the waterside. But in newly built gardens or scenic areas, trees very different from weeping willows in shape and characteristics such as the metasequoia and the black poplar are used to equal advantage (figure 3-18). The upward grandeur of the canopy lines formed by groves of these tall trees contrasts with the flat water surface to form a balanced artistic composition. A single tall tree by the side of a large water surface may look awkward. However, the grouping of the trees should harmonize with the style of the garden and the immediate environment. For instance, in Hangzhou's West Lake, there is a famous scenic spot named "Three Pools Mirroring the Moon". The major trees there are sturdy willows with spreading branches (figure 3-19). Over the centuries, these trees have become an integral part of the scenery, and people are so familiar with them that replacement by other trees such as metasequoia would destroy the traditional setting.

In planning the vegetation on the banks of wide water surfaces, attention should be paid to the canopy line as it may appear to those boating in the water. The alternate planting of two different kinds of trees can make an undulating and rhythmic canopy line. Figure 3-20a presents an example of the alternate planting of weeping willows and camphor trees. They are different in shape and colour. The former have swaying branches and are in light green whereas the latter look sturdy and are in deep green. The canopy line undulates gracefully along the curved bank of the lake in harmonious colour. If a pond is used mainly for raising waterfowls, the canopy line of the plants on the bank can be made more simple. If there are buildings by the waterside, it is advisable to grow many different trees and shrubs so as to form an interesting contour line involving the buildings and the plants (figure 3-20b). If the waterside buildings are the major scene with the plants playing an offsetting role, the vegetation should match with the buildings in shape and quantity, and form a balanced contour line.

When there are scenic views on the other side of the water surface, they must not be blocked from sight by waterside vegetation. Figure 3-21 shows the view of a giant banyan tree in perspective on the opposite bank as seen from a bamboo grove in a natural scenic area. If the bamboos were too densely grown, the perspective would be lost. The attraction on the other bank could also be a pavilion, a hill or a panoramic view, in which case large shady trees planted at wide intervals will form a frame to put the view in proper perspective (figure 3-22a). Sometimes, as shown in figure 3-22b, a single large tree can produce similar results. The southern magnolia by the side of a medium-sized water surface has a crown 5 m wide and 1.5 m above ground, providing excellent shade for the bench underneath. Viewed from the "hooded" enclave, the waterside scenery on the opposite bank looks

Figure 3-18   Towering black poplars and weeping willows are grown on either side of the water for contrast.

Figure 3-19   The traditional way of planting waterside willow trees in China.

Figure 3-18

Figure 3-19

*igure 3-20 a

exceptionally clean and bright under the sun. To serve the purpose, the tree chosen should be broad-leaved and have thick foliage to create an aura of seclusiveness.

One of the functions of a water surface is the reflecting of shadows which virtually double the image of the waterside scene, and increase the depth of the vista. Reflections in the water reduce the varying dimensions of land objects into one flat image. It looks different every time it is viewed from a different angle, which makes it extremely fascinating. In addition, a clear, light green water surface can bring the colours of the waterside scenes into harmony. Since the colour of the water and the green foliage of trees on the bank are close to each other and may appear monotonous, it is desirable to choose plants in rich colours. The reflections of reds, yellows and oranges are especially striking in clear waters.

The following is an analysis of the plant disposition around a pond in a garden (figure 3-23). The water surface is divided into two parts by a bridge. The major part is 1.5 hectare, or 5/6th of the whole area. The smaller part is surrounded by big trees and other plants, and there are a lot of water plants in the pond. Thus a closed-in water scene is formed in contrast to the openness of the adjoining larger water surface. There a small island of about 180 m² is set in the south, which has the role of centralizing the scenes and separating and increasing the depth of vision—a method often used in the designing of classical Chinese gardens. The merits of the planting scheme are apparent in several ways:

1. The plants are not uniformly grown around the banks but at various distances from the water. Sometimes a lawn stretches out into the water, broadening the vision. The groves of trees on the banks vary in density, and people following the winding path find themselves sometimes close to the water and sometimes deep in the woods, which enhances the attraction of the water vistas.

2. The large lawns around the pond serve to scatter the crowds near the water.

3. In choosing the shrubs and trees, attention is given to seasonal scenic changes. Planted by the water under the trees and near the lawns are large tracts of azaleas mixed at random with cherry trees, camellias and yulan magnolias to add a touch of spring. In summer, the scenery is enhanced with a few crapemyrtles and silk trees set against a background of oriental sweetgums and broad-leaved evergreens. In the southeast are tracts of maples whose red foliage marks the advent of autumn. The planting of snow azaleas instead of red flowering plants beside the maples makes a good colour combination.

4. The five cherry trees on the south bank of the pond creates a fascinating scene in combination with the landscape, the paths and other plantings. Seen from one angle, the bright cherry flowers are framed in large evergreen trees. When seen from another angle, the five cherry trees, being not on a straight line, look like a small wood. Viewed from still another angle, one can only enjoy the beauty of a single cherry tree, for the vision line is blocked by the evergreen groves. By the time the sightseer emerges from the cherry grove, a new delightful vista appears before the eye. The arrangement of these five cherry trees is the result of careful planning.

Figure 3-20 Waterside canopy line and contour line.

a. Canopy line formed by weeping willows and camphor trees.

b. Sketch: Contour lines formed by trees and buildings.

*igure 3-20 b

Figure 3-21

Figure 3-22 a

Figure 3-21   An opening in the waterside shrubs to allow visual enjoyment of the large tree on the opposite bank.

Figure 3-22   Vistas of distant scenery from under shady trees which function like a huge lens hood.

a. A panoramic view of the opposite bank as seen from under the shelter of oriental plane trees.

b. The scenery on the opposite bank appears brighter and clearer when viewed from a shady spot on this side of the water.

Figure 3-22 b

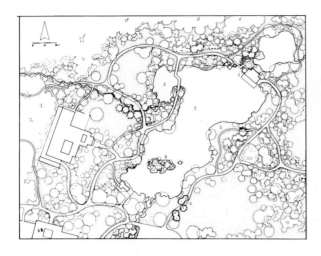

Figure 3-23 *a*

Figure 3-23 *c*

Figure 3-23 *b*

Figure 3-23   An example of plant disposition for space near water.

a. Plan: 1. Waterside pavilion. 2. The main water area. 3. A smaller water area. 4. Cherry blossoms. 5. A small lawn protruding toward the water. 6. A little island.

b. Spring scenery around the main water area.

c. Autumn scenery at the waterside pavilion.

d. The five cherry trees on the southern bank of the main water area.

Plantings for Garden Buildings

Chapter Four

Plantings for Garden Buildings

Plants and buildings are both component parts of a garden scenery. Many Chinese gardens known for their scenic splendour, are often named after, and distinguished by, specific buildings. At West Lake in Hangzhou, there is a scenic spot known as "Enjoy the singing orioles amid waving willows," so named because there, weeping willows are planted in great abundance. However, the major scene consists of a pavilion housing a tablet and the "listening-to-oriole" hall, both flanked by willow trees to correspond to the name of the spot (figure 4-1). At the Tomb of Yue Fei, a loyal general in the 12th century, there stands a large wall on which are the words: "He served his country with unreserved loyalty." Along the wall are rows of azaleas, whose flaming red flowers are meant to be a token of sorrow for, and respect to, the hero who was wrongly executed by the emperor. Azaleas imply a miscarriage of justice from still another angle. It happens that azalea and cuckoo are mononyms in Chinese. Legend has it that the soul of King of Shu (c. 770 B.C.), who died in great sorrow, turned into a cuckoo which "chirps long and sadly until its mouth bleeds." The planting of azaleas at the Tomb is a typical example that the vegetation around a building corresponds with the purpose for which the building was constructed. In some cases, proper plant disposition can bring into harmony the buildings and their surrounding environment. For instance, when a building or a group of buildings are too large or too small, or are strange-looking, partly damaged, dull in colour or awkwardly situated, well-designed plantings can produce a compensatory effect. The buildings in figure 4-2a are too high and extended to match with the garden scenery in front of them. The designer overcame the disharmony by screening the buildings with four large camphor trees. In gardens, when functional buildings are too prominently situated to be in harmony with the scenery, they should be screened by trees in the same manner.

Most buildings are straight or geometric in form, but plants and their branches bend naturally. A dynamic balance can be achieved by properly matching the plants with the buildings. For example, a bamboo grove or a plum tree with their stems and branches slightly inclining toward a moon gate make up an attractive combination of lines and forms. With the shadows of the bamboos flickering on the white wall, the moon gate appears more fascinating (figure 4-2b).

The green foliage of trees serves well as a medium that harmonizes the various colours of the buildings. Since the walls of most buildings are light in colour, they make excellent background for the colour of the flowers, leaves and trunks of different trees and shrubs. When the colour of the walls is too light to set off light-colour flowers or shrubs, it is preferable to choose tall plants so that the flowers will appear above the walls against a blue sky (figure 4-3).

The combination of buildings and plants also requires harmony in style. If cone-shaped Norfolkisland pines are grown in front of traditional Chinese buildings, they will obviously look inharmonious. However, the same trees will blend well with buildings in Western style.

In an area dominated by buildings, plants which change with seasons can give a vivid and variable appearance to an otherwise dull and monotonous scene. In summertime, thick

Figure 4-1

Figure 4-1 At this pavilion named "Enjoy the Singing Orioles amid Wavy Weeping Willows," willow trees are grown in abundance and matched by peach trees. The pink peach blossoms together with green willows symbolize the advent of spring in traditional Chinese literature.

Figure 4-2 a

Figure 4-2 b

Figure 4-2   Using plants to soften the architectural appearance of buildings.

a. The large camphor trees in front of the buildings bring harmony to environs.

b. Using green bamboo to shelter the white wall and a plum tree to accent the moon gate makes the scene look harmonious in colour and lines.

Figure 4-3

Figure 4-4 b

Figure 4-4 Decoration of entrances to garden exhibits.

a. The entrance to an exhibit of bonsai. A huge bonsai is placed immediately inside the moon gate to indicate the theme.

b. The entrance to a chrysanthemum show. Espalier chrysanthemums decorate the left side of the gate; tiny potted chrysanthemums at the upper right corner of the entrance form two Chinese ideograms meaning "enjoy the chrysanthemums."

Figure 4-4 a

Figure 4-5

foliage makes the space appear shaded and compact; while in winter, bare trees make the same area appear more spacious and bright. Additionally, plant disposition should match the building's functional and artistic requirements. For instance, for religious buildings, large, long-lived and ancient-looking trees are preferable. For buildings marking road directions or for small picturesque structures like a roadside pavilion, it is desirable to match them with plants that have colourful flowers and attractive leaves. Thick groves and hedges are suitable for keeping a garden quiet and secluded.

In short, it is unthinkable that buildings, especially those in a garden, are left to stand alone without decorative vegetation.

I. Plant Arrangements at the Entrance

The appearance of a garden entrance should bear distinctive features that give expression to the particular theme and style of the garden. Usually at the entrance are facilities such as ticket office, refreshment stalls and a small pavilion or bench for people to rest or wait for friends. A common public garden should appear pleasant at the entrance, while a particular type of garden requires specific distinctive accents. The entrance to a temple garden, for example, should bear an atmosphere of antiquity, plainness, serenity and a mystic air. The entrance to the courtyard of a home, however, should be direct and appear inviting. Thus, the plant disposition at garden entrance could be artistic or plain, depending on the purpose it serves.

At some gardens, the entrance is a flower pergola with climbing plants such as wistaria. Potted chrysanthemum or cypress are artfully displayed underneath the latticework to lend colour when the wistarias fade away. However, a pergola is not a permanent set-up. It is good as a transitional device or a supplement to permanent buildings at the entrance.

The plantings at the entrance of a special garden are usually an indication of the garden's theme. Figure 4-4a shows an entrance to a garden mainly consisting of potted miniature plants and landscapes. The horizontal inscription above the moon gate meaning "Garden of Assorted Landscapes" and a large miniature landscape model right inside the entrance clearly indicate the nature of the garden.

In many Chinese cities, exhibitions of potted chrysanthemum are held every autumn. At the entrance of these exhibitions, various varieties of chrysanthemum are displayed in attractive patterns. There are also garden entrances decorated with a kind of climbing chrysanthemum which looks tasteful by itself (figure 4-4b).

On festival days in China, immediately inside the garden entrance are large artfully designed flower beds composed of potted flowers in striking colours. Sometimes the design expresses a certain theme. When the festival is over, the potted flowers are easily removed, and the entrance restored to its normal appearance. This method of creating a festive atmosphere at garden entrances has become a tradition in China.

In natural scenic areas, the entrance is often marked by an archway, a pavilion, a massive gate or a tiled screen. Usually an archway is built among trees, and therefore its size and shape should match the natural environment. Figure 4-5 shows the archway that leads to the Gushan scenic area near Fuzhou, Fujian Province. It stands in the midst of a grove of masson pines in the mountains.

In China, ancient temples are found in all famous mountains. The plantings at the entrance of a temple can strengthen the religious atmosphere. Figure 4-6 shows the gateway to a Daoist monastery. A couplet painted in blue eulogizing the eternal continuity of Daoism and the greatness of its founder Lao Zi flank the gate. The walls on either side of the

Figure 4-5 A memorial archway built in the mountains. Its tall structure and distinctive lines are matched with the shape of the surrounding trees.

entrance are painted a bright yellow. In front of the gateway are a number of evergreens including one camphor tree, one glossy privet, one masson pine, two evergreen chinkapins and two Chinese parasol trees, forming colour combinations of green, yellow and blue. The overhanging branches of the camphor tree slanting above the gateway add charm to the monastery entrance.

Some ancient temples do not have a gate but use a tiled screen to mark the entrance. Figure 4-7 shows one of these screening walls. The Chinese characters meaning "The western paradise is within reach" inscribed on the wall shows that behind the screen is a Buddhist temple. Beside the screen is a huge old camphor tree without any flowering plants around. The imposing screen, painted in pink and bearing the gilded characters, is "framed" in the verdant foliage of the tree, adding dignity to tranquility in complete harmony with the aura of an ancient temple.

In some gardens, there are small buildings or enclosed courtyards used as living quarters. It is desirable to grow some climbing evergreen or flowering plants at the entrance to decorate the door and walls (figure 4-8a). A flower pergola at the entrance, such as the one in figure 4-8b, serves well to tone down the lighting contrast between inside and outside, besides embellishing the plain walls of the house (figure 4-8b). Sometimes, rows of white common lilac at an entrance make up a "fragrant path" leading to the gate. This arrangement is easier and produces good effects (figure 4-8c). There are also entrances which are completely shaded by plants of natural beauty.

II. Plantings at the Foot of Buildings

Chinese garden designs stress plant disposition around the base of a building, which includes the foot of walls, the corners of the house, the doors and windows, the doorsteps, and the grounds immediately around the building. These plants take a transitional role between the building and its surroundings.

Plants at the foot of walls are not only adornments. They exercise the function of consolidating the foundations of the buildings. Figure 4-9a shows a hedge of Chinese littleleaf box trees at the foot of a round building, with dwarf lilyturf grown along the edges of the circular walkway. The trees and grass form a transition from the wall to the walkway, looking like a green decorative border between the light-yellow pavement and the orange wall. Thinly planted between the hedge and the grass are enticing faber maples which add variations to the dull architectural outlines of the buildings. However, the simplest way of dressing up the foot of a wall is to grow dwarf lilyturf along it as shown in figure 4-9b. Buildings that form part of the scenery are commonly accompanied by decorative flowers or trees. For example in figure 4-10a, along a long and narrow passage are planted three crapemyrtles which have long flowering periods, and some plantain bananas at the corners of the buildings. A bamboo grove facing the passage provides a plain setting in harmony with the rest of the scene. Figure 4-10b shows still another pattern with peach trees planted on one side of the building and Manchu rose on the other, delighting sightseers with flowers in both spring and summer.

To round off sharp turns at the corners of a building and to avoid obstructing walkers, the usual way is to grow a single flowering tree on the spot. Figure 4-11a shows a Chinese redbud at the corner of a house which makes the spot more interesting. In figure 4-11b, the branches of a Chinese redbud bending toward the water extend the spread of the blossoms to form a "flower corner," making the pavilion more attractive.

Figure 4-6   This monastery entrance is marked by a tricolour combination of blue couplet boards, yellow walls and green foliage.

Figure 4-7   A green screening wall at the entrance of a Buddhist temple bearing four Chinese characters meaning "The Western Paradise Is Within Reach" as viewed through a "frame" of the large camphor trees.

Figure 4-8 a

Figure 4-8   Plant disposition at the entrance of small courtyard gardens.

a. Espaliers on lintel and walls.

b. A flower-framed porch.

c. Sketch: Lilacs lining the passage to the entrance.

Figure 4-6

Figure 4-7

Figure 4-8 b

Figure 4-8 c

Sometimes, a single trunk or a grove of well-trimmed leafy sweet viburnum are grown around the corner to form a "green column" that hides the sharp edge (figure 4-11c). But in Chinese gardens, the most common way to decorate corners is to grow bamboo groves or to combine them with rockeries (figure 4-11d).

When lining the foot of the walls with plants, attention should be paid to the interplay of colours between the plants and the wall surface. The flowers or trees so planted should not have the same colour as the walls. For example, in figure 4-12, the colour contrast between the yellow Manchu rose and the red wall is striking. If red peach blossoms are grown there, their colour would be obscured.

Since there are large trees in most gardens, vegetation around the foot of the trees deserves special attention. The usual plants used to cover the ground around the trees include the creeping oxalis, garden pansy and ivy (figure 4-13). However, for antique trees that bear special features, individual treatment is required. Figure 4-14 shows an old camphor tree which stands in the center of a square. The lower part of the trunk is hollow. So a 5.2-m-wide platform is built around it and planted with dwarf lilyturf. Together with rockery, the tree is well-protected and is a scenic spot in itself.

III. Arrangement for Climbing Plants

The use of climbing plants is a usual way of dressing up a building, and since these plants grow in crevices on the walls, they have great potential for increasing the vegetation area without taking up extra land space. Climbing plants grow fast, with a wide adaptability to various soils and less susceptibility to diseases and insect pests. They are also easy to reproduce, mostly by cuttings. In quiet corners in gardens or in enclosed courtyards for office workers, climbing plants such as grapevine, pea or squash are grown which are not only beautiful to look at but also practical. Climbing plants also have a climatizing function. Tests have shown that in summertime, the surface temperature of walls covered with Japanese creepers is 5°C lower than that without any covering plants, and surface dust is reduced by 20 percent. Buildings draped with climbing plants blend well with natural environment. In Chinese gardens, there are scores of climbing plants used mainly for decorating walls, roofs, doors and windows, as well as trellises and flower corridors.

It should be added, however, that vertical vegetation isn't needed on all kinds of buildings, especially structures that are works of art themselves. To cover them with creeping plants would mar architectural beauty.

Here are some examples of the dispositions for climbing plants:

Figure 4-15a shows a building covered with Japanese creepers that harmonize with the surrounding green environment. Figure 4-15b shows a pergola mantled with the same plant. The thick foliage provides a shady and cool resting place.

The wistaria trellis in figure 4-16a in the Summer Palace, Beijing, is a common feature in classical Chinese gardens. It is characterized by copious tangled vines and flowerage. In modern gardens, wistaria is also grown in front of buildings for special purposes. For instance in figure 4-16b, the overhanging wistarias reduce light reflection through the windows and modify the dull lines of the window frames. At the foot of the building are two pruned hedges of Chinese littleleaf box trees that make the building look neat and sturdy.

The trellised Chinese trumpet creepers in figure 4-17 are in the Shanghai Botanical Garden. The starry red flowers look particularly attractive.

Grapevine is very common in parks. Figure 4-18 shows a pergola of grapevines in the Zhongshan Park, Beijing. Clusters of luscious grapes never fail to attract people, but for a garden, they should be kept within limits.

Figure 4-9 a

Figure 4-9 b

Figure 4-9 Examples of plantings at the foot of buildings.

a. The Chinese littleleaf box trees along the walls and the dwarf lilyturf lining the foot of the walls provide a transition between the walls and the walkway.

b. Planting dwarf lilyturf is a simple way of decorating the foot of a wall.

Figure 4-10 Plant disposition in front of buildings in courtyards.

a. Crapemyrtles grace the front of the buildings; the white wall on the right is sheltered by the large green leaves of plantain bananas.

b. A setting that displays peach blossoms in spring and Manchu rose in summer.

Figure 4-10 a

Figure 4-10 b

Figure 4-11 Plant disposition around house corners.

a. Chinese redbud at the corner of a wall adds colour to uninteresting angular lines.

b. Sketch: Sweet-scented oleanders at the corner of a pavilion enriches the scene. Some of the branches bend downward in contrast to the upturned eaves of the pavilion.

c. Sweet viburnum softens the angle at the corner of the house.

d. Bamboo and rockeries at a sharp corner between two walls cover up an ugly spot.

Figure 4-11 a

Figure 4-11 b

Figure 4-11 c

Figure 4-11 d

Figure 4-12

Figure 4-12   Yellow flowers go well with a red wall.

Figure 4-13   Tricolour viola cover an otherwise bare ground round a tree.

Figure 4-14

Figure 4-15 a

Figure 4-14   Rockeries set at the foot of an ancient tree form a pleasant little scene.

Figure 4-15 b

Figure 4-15   The decorative Peking ivy.

a. A green wall surface in harmony with the surroundings.

b. A green pergola provides a shady resting place.

Figure 4-16 a

Figure 4-16   A climbing plant —wistaria.

a. The kind of flower trellis often seen in Chinese classical gardens.

b. Overhanging wistarias decorate dull window frames.

Figure 4-17   A climbing plant —Chinese trumpet creepers.

Figure 4-16 b

IV. Plantings for Small Structures

In most Chinese gardens are found pavilions, long corridors, trellises, small bridges, statues, engraved tablets, even chairs and lampposts which are artistically designed and play a decorative role. But they still need to be matched with plantings, especially for small functional buildings which would otherwise appear dull and isolated.

Pavilions, sometimes surrounded by water, and corridors are very common in Chinese gardens. There are more than one hundred such pavilions around West Lake in Hangzhou. They can be classified into eight categories: tablet pavilions, memorial pavilions, mountain pavilions, water pavilions, roadside pavilions, tea pavilions, doorway pavilions and flower pavilions. The plant disposition for these different pavilions should meet the requirements of their major functions.

A tablet pavilion should be built at a place where people usually pass by. The plantings nearby should be simple, often consisting of one or two large trees to provide shade and enhance the artistic effect. Figure 4-19 is one such pavilion 5 m high and surrounded by willows. Two trunks of *Prunus persica var duplex* are grown about 10 m from the pavilion. Around March, the red flowers amid green leaves present a charming scene. Two camphor trees frame the pavilion at a distance.

The choice and disposition of plants beside a memorial pavilion should be in tune with the person(s) commemorated. The famous Chinese hermit Lin Bu (967-1028) of the Song Dynasty once lived at Gushan Mountain near Hangzhou. He planted a plum tree to commemorate his wife and treated the cranes he raised as his sons. After his death, people built "Fang He Ting" (a pavilion to train cranes) by the water near the mountain and set up a tablet to record the story. A camphor tree over 20 m tall with an extensive canopy stands by the pavilion. The foothill at the back of the pavilion is planted with groves of plum trees. The whole setting serves well to interpret the plain and elevated taste of the ancient hermit (figure 4-20).

Figure 4-20

Figure 4-18

Figure 4-18   A grape trellis.

Figure 4-19

Figure 4-19 A tablet pavilion stands out through the "frame" of two large camphor trees.

A roadside pavilion is often built at a spot where people are likely to pause for a rest. All kinds of trees and shrubs can be grown around it. Figure 4-21 shows such a pavilion on the fringe of a lawn with a path leading to it. The pavilion and the surrounding trees dominate the lawn. The trees consist of osmanthus and cypress. A single 15-m-high glossy privet and some rockeries help to keep the pavilion from looking bare and exposed. A few red-leafed Japanese maples add variation to colour.

For a waterside pavilion, the plant disposition should be in harmony with the shape and size of the body of water and the composition of the surrounding trees and their colours. In figure 4-22, the pavilion is set beside a small pond surrounded by hills. The sightseer first gets a bird's eye view of the pavilion and the water from a hilltop path in the shade of a large camphor tree, whose foliage creates a picture frame which accentuates the prominence of the sun-lit pavilion down below. Planted around the pavilion are low groves of Japanese maples, pomegranates, plum trees, Chinese littleleaf box trees and nandinas. In such a setting, the pavilion should not be too large so as to harmonize with the limited water area. Since the water surface must be visible from inside the pavilion, its foundation is raised to consist of two tiers, and since the pavilion is framed in by large trees on the surrounding slopes, it is important to grow only low tree groves close to the pavilion to avoid obscuring the central point of interest.

A mountain pavilion, of course, is usually located on wooded mountainsides. To match

Figure 4-20 "Crane-training Pavilion" on the bank of a wide water surface. It is so named to commemorate ancestors who are believed to have trained cranes here. Trees are grown sparsely around the pavilion to clear the way for cranes.

Figure 4-21

Figure 4-22

Figure 4-21 A rich variety of plants partially hide the wayside pavilion.

Figure 4-23 A pavilion tucked away in a natural mountain forest. The broad-leaved loquat tree in front of it serves as a landmark for travellers.

Figure 4-23

Figure 4-22 The size of the pavilion and its roof are in proportion and the trees on the elevated grounds around form a "picture frame."

the surrounding environment, the pavilion should be plain rather than ornate. For example in figure 4-23, the pavilion is built in the midst of a forest of secondary *Cyclobalanoposis glauca* of the oak family. The serene setting is interposed by a single loquat tree planted beside the pavilion to mark its location. The structure itself is simple in style, with no decoration except a piece of inscribed board. The pavilion appears natural and inviting to those who wish to sit in and enjoy the beauty of the mountain scenery.

A tea pavilion provides convenience to those who wish to take a rest and have tea while enjoying the scenery. The plantings around this kind of pavilion should be less dense, with spaces to relish the surrounding sceneries. Trees with long flowering periods and thin trunks are preferred to those that shed fruits or leaves and are susceptible to diseases or insect pests.

A flower pavilion should be accompanied by flowers and trees that tally with the name of the pavilion. For instance, a "peony pavilion" should be matched with peonies, and a "pavilion of lotus fragrance," with lotus flowers. Attention should be paid to the seasonal features of the plants used. Sometimes it is good to grow different plants in quantity to form a scene of rich colour and texture. Sometimes, a single kind of famous flower or tree is chosen to attract people.

A doorway pavilion is used mainly for a landmark, or for service purposes, such as a ticket office. It is better to choose plants that have some connections with the garden theme besides providing shade.

Generally speaking, large arboreous trees with egg-shaped or vertical canopies are preferred to match pavilions. The beautiful egg-shaped canopy of a glossy privet, a camphor tree, a Chinese soapberry, a locust tree or a purpleblow maple overhanging part of the pavilion's roof softens the linear outlines of the pavilion. The vertical-shaped canopies such as those of oriental sweetgums, furry bamboo and ginkgo have upward branches and straight trunks. When a pavilion is built beside these trees, such as the one shown in figure 2-17b, the contrast between the low pavilion and the three tall sweetgums achieves a special effect for enjoyment.

Corridors have similar ornamental values as pavilions in a garden, but they also have the function of a passageway. They are actually garden paths with a roof. The plant disposition for corridors is also part of the garden design. If the corridor is too long, it is generally necessary to grow some flowering shrubs along it. The spacing of these shrubs should take into consideration the conditions on either side of the corridor. At sectors where the scenery is impressive, the planting scheme should leave ample space for the sightseer to enjoy the scene, and along uninteresting segments, the shrubs could be planted at much closer range. The variations can overcome the monotony of a lengthy walkway (figure 4-24). However, for special corridors such as a galley built along a wall with interesting inscriptions on it, lighting becomes important. It would be undesirable to grow tall trees with large canopies that would cut down lighting. But on the other hand, low flowering shrubs would not be adequate to keep the galley separate and quiet. The choice would be arboreous trees with small canopies or larger shrubs but not too large to block off the sun. A long corridor built in a natural forest should be made to wind through the woods to enhance its appeal.

Most small bridges in gardens are themselves artistic structures that need little embellishment by ornamental plants. But some of these bridges are not prominently located, and two or three stands of colourful plants close by can serve as a direction guide (figure 4-25). Some bridges demand a full plant setting to attract tourists besides their own beautiful shapes. For instance, in figure 4-26, a tranquil "bridgehead with flowers" is formed by growing banks rose on a trellis.

Figure 4-24

Figure 4-24   Flowering plants on one side of a long walkway relieves tediousness.

Figure 4-25

Figure 4-25   Faber maples mark a bridgehead.

Figure 4-26

Figure 4-26 The dense flowering trellis at the end of a bridge leads the sightseer on to what is in store ahead.

Plantings for statues in gardens should provide the right background, particularly in colour combination. Figure 4-27 shows the statue of Mr. Cai Yuanpei (1868-1940), formerly president of the Beijing University. The foundation is white and the statue is bronze with evergreen pines in the background. This combination symbolizes the immortal spirit of Mr. Cai through colour contrast between the statue and its foundation. Grown asymmetrically on either side of the statue are red-leaved myrobalan plums and deodar cedars with a wide lawn in front. This asymmetrical and natural style of the layout symbolizes Mr. Cai's open mind and his spirit in fighting feudalism and embracing democracy and freedom. Attention should also be paid to the space around a statue when using large trees. When the statue stands at the end of a long field of vision, the trees should be grown at a suitable distance from the statue, about two to three times the height of the figure. This is to form a "picture frame" with the trees' foliage to accentuate the view of the statue. Generally speaking, it is preferable to keep the vegetation around a garden statue natural and full of life. And it is better to choose those plants that have some bearing on what the statue represents.

Benches are common small objects in gardens. They not only give people a resting place but also provide vantage points for enjoying views. The plant disposition at these points should permit people not only to enjoy the scenery in the distance and flowers nearby, but also provide shade in the summer and sunlight in the winter. When such seats are set under trees, large deciduous trees are preferred to others because the extensive canopies can function as a "lens hood" that puts distant views in sharper focus. Placing low seats under large trees can also increase the sense of broadness and may even bring about a wild mountain forest atmosphere. For example in figure 4-28a, some stone tables and stools are naturally scattered under a large camphor tree. The stone table is less than 1 m high in strong contrast to the tall tree. From here, one gets the feeling of being part of the natural scene with the lake and the distant mountains. However, nearby along the same lake, a Japanese maple and two glossy privets of moderate stature in a triangle and some rockeries combine to form a small tranquil space which provides a viewpoint in the shade (figure 4-28b). The two lakeside retreats create quite different atmospheres, which shows the effects of plantings even on small garden objects like benches.

Figure 4-27 Evergreens of different varieties add dignity to the bust of Cai Yuanpei (1868-1940), noted Chinese educator.

Figure 4-27

Figure 4-28 a

Figure 4-28   Plantings near garden seats.

a. Putting stone tables and seats underneath a large tree 20 times over in height provides both clear view and shade.

b. A seat in thick shade is suitable for enjoyment of scenery in the distance.

c. A seat among flower bushes facilitates enjoying the plants at close range.

When seasonal flowers are grown for enjoyment, it is best to build benches amid the plants. Figure 4-28c shows a bench under three yulan magnolias. When in full bloom, they diffuse fragrance that creates a beautiful environment for enjoyment. For plants grown around benches, it is better to choose the flowery and sweet-smelling varieties such as the silk tree, cherry tree, osmanthus, yulan magnolia, lilac, crapemyrtle, banana shrub and wintersweet. Putting benches under small trees should be avoided because of interference with the vision line. And flowery plants should be kept away from the seats.

Generally speaking it is unnecessary to grow ornamental plants near man-made objects that are attractive by themselves. However, if the objects are poorly designed, they can benefit from some decoration with plants. Figure 4-29 shows wistaria winding around a plain lamppost and turning it into a "lamp tree." It is particularly attractive in the flowering season.

Figure 4-29 Espaliered wistaria on a
lamppost blends in with nearby plants

Figure 4-28 b

Figure 4-28 c

128

Flower Beds

Chapter Five

Flower Beds

Besides growing flowers in everyday life or in gardens of special interests, the Chinese people like to hold flower festivals or flower shows with seasonal characteristics. Another favourite art of plant growing is the cultivation of bonsai which can live very long, some keeping green as long as five to six hundred years. However, in gardens, the cultivation of flower beds is one of the most common and popular forms of flower cultivation. Many ancient flower beds in China used white marble as foundations, which were called *Xu Mi Zuo* (figure 5-1). Modern flower beds have many different styles. Generally speaking, those with flowers as their main feature are called flower beds, whereas those covered mainly by trees, grass and herbaceous plants are named plant beds (figure 5-2). In places where there are no permanent foundations, a flower bed is formed simply by putting together potted flowers in various patterns.

Flower beds are mainly for enjoyment and decoration. Nowadays, all kinds of sparkling flower beds are found in city gardens, along the streets and lanes, as well as in factories, schools and the compounds of various institutions. These flower beds, which are designed to match the environment, are usually composed of one or several kinds of flowers either arranged in geometrical patterns or left in a natural state and graded according to height. As an expression of the urban people's aesthetic senses, they are easy to handle, and along with urban development, flower beds are becoming more and more popular and elaborate.

I. Types of Flower Beds

Flower beds take many shapes, such as round, elliptic, square, belt-shaped and polygonal. They are found at the entrance of gardens, in front of buildings, in the centre of courtyards, around house corners, alongside walls, under trees, along roads or on safety islands. Some look like a platform, others look like a staircase or a giant bouquet. The flowering time varies from one to four seasons, and some beds last for merely one flowering period. The following is an introduction to the various styles and functions of flower beds.

Flat, patterned flower beds. These are terraces covered with various herbaceous flowers and grass or with the multi-colour copper alternanthera arranged in geometric patterns, with some more complicated than others (figure 5-3a). The planting is done in rings slightly different in height. These are the most widely used in various surroundings, and are particularly suitable for slanting surfaces or for viewing from a higher position. Those flower beds using copper alternanthera along with other herbs to form complicated patterns are known as "floral blanket" terraces (figure 5-3b).

Stereoscopic or ornamental flower beds. The pattern follows a specific design or expresses a definite theme, such as a 3-dimensional image of a flower vase, a pavilion, a giant panda, a peacock, a sea lion or some other objects. Such terraces are often located in the centre of a garden or in front of a large public building. The choice of motif depends on the environment and subject requirement (figure 5-4).

Statue flower beds. These are made up of herbaceous flowers and grass or evergreen plants which match with the statues or rockeries set on the terrace. The statue usually expresses a

Figure 5-1   A classical flower bed on a white marble base.

Figure 5-2   A plant bed mixing herbaceous flowers and trees.

Figure 5-1

Figure 5-2

motif and is strongly ornamental. For example, in the "Fish-Watching Garden" in Hangzhou, there is a flower bed with a red carved wooden fish standing upright in the centre. The statue points up the theme of the garden and serves as a landmark for tourists as well (figure 5-5a).

Some gardens do not have fixed flower beds. They make patterned flower piles at certain scenic spots during festivals to heighten the holiday atmosphere (figure 5-5b.c.). If a natural rock should be used as the motif, it must usually have ornamental values in shape and colour (figure 5-5d).

Supportive flower beds. These are built at the foot of walls, around corners of buildings, in front of windows or entrances, or on both sides of flights of steps mainly for decorative purposes. Flower beds along the foot of walls create ornamental edges which play a transitional role. Those around the corners of buildings make the surroundings look more beautiful, and sometimes cover up structural defects. In figure 5-6a, for example, a small flower bed is built between the wistaria pergola and the doorway. It fills a need for both structural balance and colour harmony. Flower beds in front of the windows of a private house help to keep the inside of the rooms out of sight and ensure privacy. Supportive flower beds should match the artistic requirements of the buildings in form and colour. But sometimes, the flower bed is a beauty in itself. Figure 5-6b shows flower beds flanking the ascending steps of a land bridge without affecting the original style of the structure. To avoid sameness with the horizontal linage of the steps, the flowers are planted in an oblique pattern. The colours of the flowers are quiet and subdued to harmonize with the flight of steps which are in a flat grey. These symmetrically arranged flower terraces are an attraction in themselves. Supportive flower beds (or flower piles) also include those that decorate trees, lampposts and advertisement signs. For example, a flower bed at the foot of a tall tree can enhance the height of the tree (Figure 5-6c), and green herbaceous plants grown around a medium-sized tree can fill up an otherwise vacant space and make the ground surface more interesting (figure 5-6d).

Figure 5-3 b

Figure 5-3 a

Figure 5-3 Designs of flower beds.

a. A design made up of flowers in various colours.

b. A design made up of copper altenanthera and common cockscomb.

Screen flower beds. These are more often found in large gardens or in front of buildings to serve as a screen or to enhance the depth of perspective or give shelter to houses. They are usually composed of flowers or trees grown on a terrace high enough to form a screen (figure 5-7).

Festival flower beds. There are set up on important festival days. They appear in many different styles and striking colours to create a pleasant and lively atmosphere. To exactly match the timing and spirit of a holiday, potted flowers are commonly used (figure 5-8).

Street flower beds. These are built mainly at crossroads, in the middle of safety islands or as separating belts on the road. Sometimes they are also built along the main paths in larger gardens (figure 5-9). These flower beds beautify a city and guide traffic. They should be in striking colour to attract attention. Usually these beds should avoid taking too much space, but those along the main paths in gardens should be large enough for enjoyment.

Pruned plant beds. These are often composed of evergreen Chinese littleleaf box trees whose thick foliage can be pruned and shaped in many ways to form decorative patterns or characters. Topiary plants like these are often set on an inclined plane as a novelty attraction.

Figure 5-4 Stereoscopic flower beds.

a. A flower basket crowning the bed to symbolize prosperity.

b. The image of phoenix symbolizes auspiciousness.

c. The image of a fairy scattering flower petals symbolizes goodness.

Figure 5-4 a

Figure 5-4 b

Figure 5-4 c

d. The image of a giant panda dominates the flower bed in front of the panda house in the Beijing Zoo.
e. A pavilion completely composed of plants suggests the advent of summer.

Figure 5-4 d

Figure 5-4 e

Figure 5-5 a

Figure 5-5 b

Figure 5-5 c

Figure 5-5 Statue flower beds.

a. A "carp" as the motif at the entrance of a fish pond.

b. A "swan" as the motif on the bank of a pond.

c. A "lion" as the motif in the imperial palace in Beijing.

d. An ornamental rock as the motif in a classical garden.

Figure 5-5 d

Figure 5-6 Supportive flower beds (including plant beds).

a. A small flower bed at the corner between two walls brightens up a dull angle.

b. The flower beds on both sides of the steps add colour and relieve the monotony of the transverse lines.

c. The flower bed makes the old hardy tree look more striking.

d. These square plant beds add green colour to the bare ground.

Figure 5-6 a

Figure 5-6 b

Figure 5-7 A flower or plant bed can serve as a partial screen.

Figure 5-8 a

Figure 5-8 Festival flower beds.
a. Flower beds composed of potted flowers at the entrance of a classical garden create a festive atmosphere for the duration of the holiday.

b. A pair of flower-decked "dragons" playing with a "pearl," China's traditional symbol for auspiciousness and happiness.

Figure 5-9 Flower beds along a garden's main walkway. Scarlet sage is grown in-between common box trees with white and yellow chrysanthemums as edgings.

II. Designs of Flower Beds

Flower beds sometimes are the centre of attraction in a garden, and sometimes merely fill spaces in between buildings. So when designing a flower bed attention should be given to its main function, particularly its relations with the surroundings.

A flower bed built in front of a building should match it in size, form and position. A flower bed should not take up more than one-third, nor less than one-fifth of the space in front of the building. To avoid pedestrian damage and facilitate drainage, border stones are used to raise the bed slightly above ground with the central part slanting evenly toward the edges. The slope angle should be less than 30°. A high terrace is not preferable because people are less able to enjoy the flower bed as a whole.

The borders of a flower bed should match the form of the base on which it is built. For instance, in figure 5-10, a round flower bed is built on a base of the same shape at the head of a bridge where pedestrians and traffic move along the circle. When flower beds are built in front of modern buildings, they can be designed in various geometric shapes. But in compounds housing ancient Chinese buildings, flower platforms should be elevated to a certain height to harmonize with the surrounding ancient buildings which usually have foundations raised three to eight steps above ground. As for the shapes of flower beds, the square, fan-shaped and round ones are more common. The choice depends on the surroundings and aesthetic requirements.

The borders of flower beds are usually 10-15 cm high, the width varies with the size of the beds. A large bed should have a wide edge. Materials for building the borders range from brick, tile, cement to high-quality terrazzo, granite, and marble. For flower beds in front of modern buildings, cement concrete, terrazzo or marble is recommended; for beds near ancient buildings, bricks, grey tiles or glazed tiles laid in a chequered pattern are preferable. The flower beds in imperial gardens are often built on white-marble foundations to match the magnificence of palace buildings. The choice of colour for the borders is to be determined by the surroundings as long as they do not overshadow the flowers. Since most ancient Chinese imperial palaces have red walls and yellow glazed tiles, and the ornamental flowers there are often very colourful, it is better to build borders with materials in plain colour such as light green or white.

Full attention should be paid to the design of patterns which should be eye-catching. The subject matter and style of the patterns should correspond with the surrounding buildings, backgrounds and statues, if any.

A flower bed in front of a building in traditional style should display designs with folk-art characteristics. For beds in imperial palaces, patterns of dragons and phoenixes are appropriate. In addition, the individual characteristics of plants should also be taken into consideration. For example, the pattern of a herbaceous flower bed should be simple and in bold outlines because these plants are uneven and are therefore unfit for fine designs. A flower bed pattern as the one in figure 5-10a is often composed of copper alternanthera which has small and bushy stems that hug the ground and tend to thicken the patterns.

The lay of flower beds is usually higher in the centre and lower on the edges, forming an inclined plane in all directions that presents a clear view from any angle (figure 5-10b). If plants of different heights are used, they should be graded evenly so as not to hinder the vision line. For large flower beds, a single trunk or a small grove of higher plants like broom cypress and common box can be grown in the midst or around the flowers that are of the same height to add variation to an otherwise flat plant composition.

Since colour scheme is the main attraction of a flower bed, contrasts and harmony as well as seasonal changes involving the flower colours should be taken into consideration.

For instance, the color of scarlet sage and that of purple cockscomb are too close to match. The former can make a better match with light green Dutch aster, and the latter with pink China aster or yellow florists chrysanthemum.

The pink daisy first appears in red, turns pink when in full blossom, and eventually becomes white. This characteristic has to be taken into consideration when mixing pink daisies with other plants in a flower bed.

Colour coordination between a flower bed and its surroundings is equally important. If the flowerage near the bed is in red in spring and white in summer, avoid similar colours in the flower bed. Another point of attention is the colour contrasts with the walls of the surrounding buildings. For example, the walls of palace buildings are mostly dark red, so the flower beds in front of them should be dominated by plain, quiet colours to avoid patchy colour clashing.

In China, like in other countries, different colours are used for different occasions. Red is the traditional colour for an auspicious occasion, and white, for mourning. Therefore, on important festival days, flower beds are mainly composed of red flowers such as scarlet sage, red cockscomb, and common poinsetta, around which yellow pink and white flowers are put as accents to enhance the holiday atmosphere. But for memorial or mourning days, white colour should predominate instead of red. As for seasonal preferences cold colours like white, blue and light green are generally preferable in summer; yellow and pink in spring, warm colours like red and purple in late autumn.

III. Choice and Disposition of Plants for Flower Beds

The basic principles in choosing plants for flower beds are: high ornamental value, long flowering time and easiness of cultivation. For beds in which herbaceous flowers predominate, annuals or biannuals like common snapdragon, potmarigold calendula and common China aster are preferable. They are colourful, branchy, leafy and graceful, have common flowering periods, and flower four times before fading. However, a spring flower bed has to be seeded in the previous autumn and protected from the winter cold which increases costs. So the use of these plants may be limited.

Perennial flower plants such as tatarian aster, Chinese pink, seal flower, day-lily and roof iris save labour. Once they are planted, they continue to grow and flower year after year and only need pruning and protection against exposure during the winter. However, since they are in blossom once a year, with only green leaves left for the rest of the time, these kinds of flower beds are built mostly in secondary places as accents. Other perennial flower plants like India canna, aztec dahlia and common tulip are also colourful and suitable for flower beds, but they have the same disadvantages as tatarian aster and others mentioned above.

Copper alternanthera is the major plant used for decorative flower beds. This plant is low and stands well to pruning. The leaves are a mixture of green, yellow, purple and red. When densely planted, they can keep the soil from erosion. If the flower bed appears dull, other colourful herbaceous plants can be added. Flower beds composed of this multi-colour herb are suitable for decorating slopes or main terraces.

Since copper alternanthera requires a temperature of over 25°C to survive the winter, it is necessary to keep the maternal plants indoors during the cold season. When the weather gets warm, cuttings are made for transplantation in fertilized shaded outdoor beds to hasten their growth. They branch in profusion, providing plenty of cuttings for transplanting in flower beds. A cutting 5 to 8 cm long will be hardy enough to transplant. The whole process involves labour and the cost is relatively high. So, for a large flower bed, turf and other colourful flower plants may be added and arranged in appropriate patterns, which will achieve equally good results.

The mature heights of the plants are an important factor in the composition of a flower bed. Their early heights are not permanent and growth may produce a height imbalance after some time. For instance in early spring, snapdragons grow slower than calendulas, but as temperature increases the former gradually grow taller than the latter. The early height of garden pansy is about the same as that of the daisy, but the former gradually outgrows the latter. Additionally, the spacing of plants involves a number of factors. Close planting induces upward growth, whereas thinning out the plants leads them to spread sideways. Therefore the spacing should be based on the mature height and spread of the plants, not the stature of their saplings. Thus, plants, with larger canopies like garden balsam and common four-o'clock should be spaced apart to avoid leggy and weak growth. However, if the plants have reached or almost reached their stable height at the time of planting, the space in-between should be kept close enough to avoid sparsity of vegetation.

The variety of plants in a flower bed is decided by the motif and the size of the bed. For a small one, three kinds of flowers are generally enough. For a large one, four to six kinds will do. The general rule should be to use whatever is needed to meet the particular artistic and conceptual requirements.

The flowering period is another important factor to consider. The same flower may have different flowering periods, depending on the locale and climate. The gardener should be able to control the time of seeding, first flowering, full flowering and the duration of the flowering periods of the various plants in the bed so as to properly stagger the periods of blooming. This is especially true of imported flowering plants settling in their new habitat.

For some flower beds, plants that have basically the same flowering period are used both for better effect and for making substitution easier. However, when plants of different flowering periods are grown in the same bed, the late-flowering kinds will provide a background for the early-flowering plants. And when the latter have faded and their withered flowers clipped, they will, in turn, serve as a background against the former. The rotation not only extends the flowering period of the bed, but also saves plants. However, this arrangement requires a thorough knowledge of the different heights, sizes and flowering periods of the plants used and a dependable timing schedule, without which the plan could very well result in confusion.

In Beijing the flower beds using herbaceous flowers generally need alterations four times a year to remain colourful and fresh. The alterations are made between the end of April and the middle of June, between the middle of June and the end of July, between early August and the middle of September and finally between middle of September and mid-October. If a flower bed is a mixture of copper alternanthera and herbaceous flowers, only the latter needs seasonal alterations. The multi-colour herb is to be pruned every month in spring and autumn. In summer three prunings are required in two months.

The length of sunshine time over the flower bed is another factor to be taken into consideration. For example, the sun-plant is in full blossom under strong sunlight but its flowers close in early mornings and evenings. The common four-o'clock, on the contrary, bursts into blossom and sends forth delicate fragrance at dawn and dusk; its flowers close in bright sunlight.

In brief, the horticultural characteristics of various flowers are the basis on which flower beds are developed for maximum enjoyment. This is the primary consideration in the designing of flower beds.

Figure 5-10   An example of a flower bed design. This one is set at the head of a bridge to guide foot and motor traffic.

a. Plan: 1. Foundation. 2. Cement edging. 3. Patterned designs. 4. Design of the centre piece.

b. Plan: Stereoscopic perspective indicating the curvature of the surface. Height diminishes evenly toward the periphery.

c. A bird's-eye view. A lamppost stands in the centre surrounded by common box and herbaceous flowers to form the centre piece which is bordered by shrubby littleleaf box trees. The ground of the bed is turfed, with copper alternanthera and common box making up the curly designs on the periphery. The edging is built with white pre-fabricated cement blocks.

Figure 5-10 a

Figure 5-10 b

Figure 5-10 c

Plantings in Courtyards and Gardens

Chapter Six

Plantings in Courtyards and Gardens

Gardens in China commonly include small courtyard gardens, larger gardens, specific flower gardens and "inner gardens." Although they vary in area, characteristics and function, the plant disposition there is always carefully designed and reflects the art of traditional Chinese gardening.

I. Plantings in Courtyards

Courtyards usually are the open space surrounded by buildings. They form an essential part of Chinese architecture. Most Chinese buildings have courtyard gardens with flowers and trees or are graced with potted flowers, regardless of the function or size of the buildings or the local climate. The plant disposition in different courtyards depends mainly on the characteristics, functions and conceptual requirements of the courtyards.

The traditional residential courtyard in north China is called a *Si He Yuan* (a quadrangular compound, which is customarily a place of elegance and tranquility. The plants grown here usually include shady Chinese locust and parasol trees; ornamental flowers like the plum, the osmanthus, the pomegranate and the Japanese kerria; fruit trees like the persimmon, the loquat, the citrus and the grape vines; and evergreens like the pine, the cypress, and the bamboo. As for disposition, they are mostly planted in pairs or singly. Figure 6-1 is a typical *Si He Yuan*. Two locust trees stand in symmetry in the north to offer shade, and two pomegranates in the south, also in symmetry, bear flowers and fruit. They combine to create a leisurely and comfortable feeling. In Chinese folklore, the locust symbolizes matchmaking and the pomegranate with its many seeds signifies numerous children. The combination of the two kinds of trees reflects China's ancient feudal family tradition.

Figure 6-2 shows an average courtyard. The entrance is in the northwest corner with lilacs grown along the side of the slated path which leads to the 60-m² main courtyard. Potted flowers and bonsai decorate the windowsills, corners round the houses, paths and top of walls. The 6-m² rectangular space fenced in by a 20-cm-high latticework facing the windowsill is a miniature rose garden with over 50 varieties of roses. There are altogether more than 150 kinds of flowers in the courtyard, including azalea, pomegranate, bracket plant, scarlet kafirlily, cape jasmine and jasmine. The two 5 x 3 m grape trellises make full use of the space. A flower cellar 1.1 m wide and 1.3 m above ground is built under the windowsill facing south. In winter, non-cold-resistant flowers are stored away in the cellar. Here, the vegetation plan and the plant management are typical of a residential courtyard with limited space.

In south China, the requirements for courtyard vegetation are different from those in the north. The high temperature and humidity in the south call for good ventilation. Turf is usually the main vegetation with some flower, flower beds or one or two shady trees on

Figure 6-1 a

Figure 6-1 Plant disposition in a typical quadrangular courtyard in China.

a. A pair of locust trees in front of south-facing rooms provide shade.

b. The two pomegranate trees in front of the north-facing rooms are for enjoyment.

Figure 6-2   The plan of a common
residential courtyard. The houses are to
the north with the courtyard in the
south and the entrance is in the
northwest corner. 1. Grape trellise. 2.
Lilacs. 3. Rose garden. 4. Green house.
5 Flowering shrubs. 6. Potted flowers. 7.
Living quarters. 8. Side rooms.

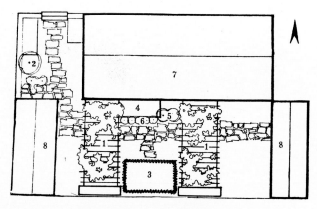

Figure 6-2

Figure 6-3

the fringes.

Courtyard planting should be in keeping with the characteristics and styles of the buildings. If the buildings are the main attraction, too much sheltering with trees is undesirable, and sometimes, it is better to have no plantings at all. For example, the grounds in the Imperial Palace in Beijing are mostly bare to fully bring out the magnificence and solemnity of the palace buildings as well as the majesty of their past. For courtyards of ordinary public premises, it is best to choose trees that are in harmony with the nature and functions of the buildings. For instance, plants that have medical value are good for the courtyards in hospitals. Yew podocarpus and bo tree are suitable for temple courtyards. The fruit of the latter can be used as beads for Buddhist rosaries. In hotel courtyards which should be restful, ornamental plants are often accompanied by other garden features. There is a hotel in scenic Guilin with a courtyard of only 20 m², which contains a pond with a sand bank, rockeries, potted plants, and bamboo. On one wall is a fresco of Guilin scenery. The whole scene is small but elegant and stands pondering about (Figure 6-3).

II. Plantings in Larger Gardens

The gardens discussed here refer to those which extend beyond the courtyards and contain other garden elements, or are attached to a certain building to serve a special purpose. These gardens are found in mansions, schools, temples and others.

Figure 6-4 is an attractive garden with residential palace buildings as the main element. It covers an area of 3,500 m . The garden is separated from the outside by humps, trees and bamboo groves at the north, west and the south. It borders on a lake in the southeast. The main characteristics of the plant disposition are as follows:

1. Creation of a tranquil residential environment by using plants to separate the space. Layers of densely-grown arboreous trees and shrubs are planted on the humps to form a screen. West of the trees is a small bamboo grove with buildings in it. At the end of a path in the grove are some black bamboos to mark the turn of the path. Some rockeries are scattered in the bamboos to accentuate natural appeal. The whole bamboo grove presents an artistic concept of simplicity and elegance which is a good example of plant disposition in this type of garden.

2. The plant arrangements on either side of the moon gate differ. The top of the gate is mantled in wistaria. There is an open lawn to the north of the gate and to the south, a grove of trees include several 3-m-high sweet osmanthus with thick foliage and ball-shaped canopies that offer good shade. Facing the gate are several sturdy southern magnolias whose leaves shine brightly in the sun. Flowering shrubs and herbaceous flowers grow on either side of the path leading to the gate. The large trees on one side of the gate and the tall bamboo grove on the other side strike an artistic balance.

3. The overall plant disposition has been given careful consideration. The garden scene is dominated by two trunks of southern magnolia nearly a hundred years old offering shade and adding serenity to the surroundings. The towering deodar cedars and masson pines form a beautiful contour line with the building. Smaller shade-tolerant trees like sweet osmanthus and camellia grow under the larger ones. Round the corners of the building are nandinas and wintersweets. Climbing plants are grown at the bridgeheads, the moon gate and the rockeries. The ground is pebbled. Sargent Chinese juniper and bamboo groves at the edges of the small lawn make a transition between the lawn and the trees and shrubs.

At the foot of the walls are planted dwarf lilyturf, which forms still another layer of green to enhance settings generally. The plant disposition in this garden gives expression

Figure 6-3 A small courtyard in a hotel in Guilin, south China.

to the traditional Chinese garden design that gives a suitable role to every element.

4. The following table lists some of the plants that have high ornamental values and are shade-tolerant and fragrant.

Name	Type	Ornamental Characteristics				Shade toler-ance	Fra-grance
		Shape of canopy	Leaf	Flower	Fruit		
Southern magnolia	evergreen arbour	O	O				
Deodar cendar	"	O					
Sweet osmanthus	evergreen small arbour			O		O	O
Winter-sweet	disiduous shrub			O			O
Dragon cypress	evergreen arbour	O					
Nandina	evergreen shrub		O		O	O	
Banks rose	semi-evergreen vine			O			O
Japanese rose	semi-evergreen vine			O			
Wistaria	deciduous vine			O			O
Sargent Chinese juniper	evergreen ground-cover						
Bamboo	evergreen						
Camellia	evergreen small arbour		O	O		O	

Figure 6-4 b

Figure 6-4 c

Figure 6-4   A residential garden with palace buildings as its main feature.

a. Plan: 1. Residential buildings. 2. Southern magnolia. 3. Masson pines. 4. Lawn. 5. A building. 6. Osmanthus. 7. Flowering shrubs. 8. Bamboo grove. 9. Winter sweets. 10. Dragon cypresses.

b. Part of the residential garden shown in the plan's lower right corner.

c. A dividing belt of trees and shrubs.

d. Sketch: A carefully-designed plant disposition with the moon gate as the focus.

Figure 6-4 a

Figure 6-4 d

Figure 6-5   A modern Chinese
residential courtyard garden.

a. Plan: 1. Camphor trees. 2. Weeping
willows. 3. Hackberry trees. 4. Southern
magnolia. 5. Chinese parasols. 6.
Chinese flowering crabapples. 7. Lawn.
8. Pond.

b. A Western-style house with a lawn.

c. A traditional Chinese garden in the
southeast corner of the layout.

d. Ornamental walls such as this
separate the sectors with completely
different scenic features.

In China, there are large residential gardens in which the living quarters are clearly separated from garden scenery. Quite a few residential gardens, both ancient and modern, belong to this type.

Figure 6-5 is a modern Chinese residential garden with an area of about 2 hectares. Its grounds are divided into three sectors by trees, buildings and walls. The west sector is residential, the buildings in the middle sector are reception halls and recreational quarters; the east sector is a garden. The open grounds in the west and middle sectors are mainly lawns. In the east sector, the northern part is completely separated from the middle sector by ornamental walls, while the southern part is bordered with trees that form part of the garden space. The buildings and lawns in the middle and west sectors are in the Western style, but right on the other side of the wall is an entirely Chinese garden with oriental waterside pavilion, zigzagging walkways, rockeries and thick groves of trees. They are informally and artfully disposed in contrast to the open lawns to the west. However, the garden is in a subordinate position, for it takes up only one-third of the whole area.

Serenity in this residential garden is achieved by bordering the entire garden and its three separate sectors by large arboreous trees such as the camphor tree, Chinese wingnut, plane tree, and smaller plants like palm and Chinese acuba. They make dense groves that keep the three sectors as independent entities. Most trees are grown in groves or rows. There are close-in areas such as the southeast corner, while the areas with lawns are open and bright. Among the 55 kinds of trees, more than half are evergreens, thus keeping much of the scenery green all the year round. However, it is a pity that only slightly more than 10 kinds of flowering plants are grown and most of these are planted singly or in pairs not enough to create an abundant flower scene. But on the whole the arrangement of plantings is good for a residential garden.

III. Plantings in Specialized Gardens

A specialized garden is one that plays up a single kind of plant in many varieties and artistically arranged. It is created mainly for enjoyment as well as to popularize botanical knowledge. These gardens can also be used to cultivate, protect or develop specific kinds of plants.

Specialized gardens appeared in China as early as the Western Han period (206 B.C.-A.D. 24).

The emperors of that time collected the plants from states west of China and also from the south, and transplanted them in their own palace gardens and entitled them "grape palace," "litchi palace" and other palaces named after the precious plants cultivated therein. Over the centuries, this kind of garden developed continuously in many versions. Some were built mainly for the enjoyment of flowers such as peony, rose, camellia and plum blossom. Some featured leafy plants like pine, cypress, bamboo, banana tree and palm. Still others gave prominence to the fruits, such as pear and loquat. There are also gardens characterized by fragrant, succulent or aquatic plants.

The areas of specialized gardens vary from several to hundreds of square meters, with some even reaching a few hectares. To set off the theme plant in a specialized garden, rockeries, ponds and other man-made structures are often added. For example the orchid garden in Guangzhou extends over an area of three hectares with more than 300 varieties. A pond, a pavilion, a bridge and ornamental walls and trees offer additional attractions to an exquisite specialized garden.

Here are the plant disposition of a few specialized gardens.

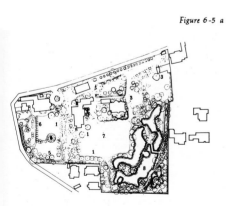

Figure 6-5 a

Figure 6-5 b

Figure 6-5 c

Figure 6-5 d

a. *Peony gardens*. In ancient China the peony was known as the flower of affluence and prestige, and was ranked as the king of flowers. It has become a tradition for the Chinese to enjoy and cherish the beauty of the peony. In the 10th century A.D., the garden at Tian Wang Courtyard in Luoyang, north China, was once a famous peony garden. According to records, the garden had "hundreds of thousands of peonies." When in full bloom, the flowerage was so luxuriant and colourful that "the whole city stopped cooking and turned out to enjoy them." In those days, peony was mainly cultivated in pots or terraces. Even to this day, in the Summer Palace near Beijing, peony terraces can still be found (figure 6-6). The terraces look plain and offer a good view, but are not very convenient for close observation.

In the last 30 years, a number of new peony gardens have been built in China. They break away from the traditional method of building a special terrace for the flowers. Instead, a series of flat flower beds one above another are carved out on hillsides adorned with rockeries. Figure 6-6 is part of a small peony garden of this type. The terraced hillsides are divided into 10 small scenic zones connected by winding 1-m-wide paths whose surface is a little lower than the flower beds. Seen as a whole, the garden remains an entity by itself without giving the impression of being sliced up by the paths. In the meantime, the paths make it possible to take a close look at the flowers wherever they are. A peony pavilion is set in the centre of the garden, and ornamental trees, particularly evergreen and colour-leaf trees, are planted to offer shade to those species which need it. Besides, the evergreens serve as the background of the peony, and the colour-leaf trees add attraction to the garden when the flowering season is over. With the peonies and background trees ingeniously arranged, the 10 zones present a variety of scenes. Some stress flowers and trees with rockeries as accents, others give prominence to the rockeries, with trees and peony combining to make an enjoyable milieu. These arrangements overcome sameness and present a whole series of different scenes to the stroller.

Not long ago, a new peony garden has been opened in the western suburbs of Beijing. Peony groves are casually scattered among natural woods (figure 6-8a). To enhance the theme, the garden features a statue of "peony goddess," a peony-shaped gateway (figure 6-8b) and a mural painting about legends connected with peony. The decorations on other buildings are all peony symbols. The appeal of the flower is everywhere.

From planting the flower in terraces in the ancient style to the modern way of cultivating peony groves in rock gardens or woods, the Chinese people have carried forward their traditional love for the peony over the centuries.

Chinese peony, an herbaceous plant, usually blooms two weeks earlier than the peony. Since the two have similar flowers, Chinese peony is often grown in peony gardens to extend the flowering period. However, it should not be given too much prominence.

b. *Medicinal herb gardens*. The medicinal herbs are both for enjoyment and for studying the characteristics and ecological features of these herbs. Figure 6-9a shows a garden of this type with an area of 1.6 hectares planted to over 1,300 kinds of medicinal herbs. The name "Medicinal Herb Garden" in Chinese characters at the entrance is formulated by clusters of Chinese littleleaf box trees. The garden features a statue of Li Shizhen (1518-1593), master of Chinese herbal medicines in the Ming dynasty, and an exhibition room entitled *Ben Cao Xuan*, meaning a studio of medicinal herbs. The studio contains potted herbs, and is named after the master's great work, *Ben Cao Gang Mu* (Compendium of Materia Medica). The garden is divided by paths into many zones. Most of these are sunny; some are shady or damp. Some are ponds, swamps or rocky grounds (figure 6-9b). Because most medicinal herbs grow in natural environment, it is necessary to create the right conditions to meet the ecological requirements of the different medicinal herbs.

For certain zones, the garden designer plants thin trees around the edges where herbs

Figure 6-6

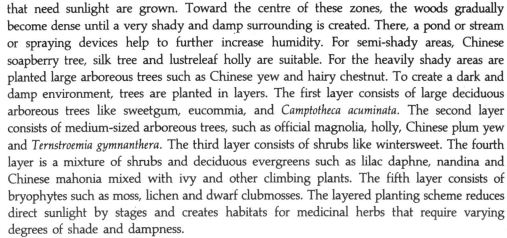

Figure 6-6   A multi-level peony terrace in the Summer Palace in Beijing. The planting design, which facilitates enjoying the flowers at close range, is inherited from ancient times.

that need sunlight are grown. Toward the centre of these zones, the woods gradually become dense until a very shady and damp surrounding is created. There, a pond or stream or spraying devices help to further increase humidity. For semi-shady areas, Chinese soapberry tree, silk tree and lustreleaf holly are suitable. For the heavily shady areas are planted large arboreous trees such as Chinese yew and hairy chestnut. To create a dark and damp environment, trees are planted in layers. The first layer consists of large deciduous arboreous trees like sweetgum, eucommia, and *Camptotheca acuminata*. The second layer consists of medium-sized arboreous trees, such as official magnolia, holly, Chinese plum yew and *Ternstroemia gymnanthera*. The third layer consists of shrubs like wintersweet. The fourth layer is a mixture of shrubs and deciduous evergreens such as lilac daphne, nandina and Chinese mahonia mixed with ivy and other climbing plants. The fifth layer consists of bryophytes such as moss, lichen and dwarf clubmosses. The layered planting scheme reduces direct sunlight by stages and creates habitats for medicinal herbs that require varying degrees of shade and dampness.

This planting plan creates a unique environment completely different from the surrounding areas. In hot and dry seasons, the temperature in the shady sector is 0.2-1°C lower than that under the sun, and the temperature in the heavily shaded and damp area is further lowered by 1.2-2°C, or sometimes by 3°C. To meet the ecological needs of different medicinal herbs in the garden, some are grown at waterside, others on rocks; some climb on other plants and some grow under thin or thick groves of trees. This way they thrive in man-made surroundings.

c. *Loquat gardens*. This is a typical kind of garden inherited from the past. Most of the trees in these gardens are loquats planted at random with other trees and matched with rockeries, pavilions and winding corridors. Figure 6-10 shows a loquat garden in south China. Its area is less than 100 m². The pavilions and corridors are in the north, east and south. The southern part of the garden is separated by walls from the rest of the garden space. Loquat trees are scattered all over the garden with one or two high, shady, deciduous trees like schneider zelkova and Chinese parasol interspersed here and there. Under the loquat trees, palms are grown to produce a layer effect. In spring the trees will be heavy with new fruit, voicing the joy of a bumper harvest.

d. *Bamboo gardens*. In China there have been quite a number of scholars and artists who have liked bamboo and enjoyed painting it almost as a hobby.

Su Shi, a Song Dynasty poet (1036-1101), wrote the following lines cherished by lovers of bamboo over the centuries: "One can manage without meat at meals, but cannot live without bamboo at home." There are many gardens in China mainly featuring bamboo. For instance, the Wang Jiang Lou Garden in Chengdu covers 12 hectares with more than 100 varieties of bamboo. Bamboo groves and bamboo paths are everywhere in this fascinating garden. A typical small bamboo garden is one called Geyuan Garden in Yangzhou, Jiangsu Province. It covers only several hundred square metres to grow bamboo used for poles. As for medium-sized bamboo gardens, they are too numerous to be individually mentioned.

These specialized gardens, emphasizing the shapes and ecological features of specific plants, possess a unique appeal of their own. Although the plants lack variety, they combine with other artistically-arranged garden elements to offer to the visitors not only enjoyment, but also knowledge about China's rich vegetation resources. The long tradition of specialized gardens is now being carried forward and continuously improved upon.

Figure 6-7 a

166

Figure 6-7   A peony rock garden.

a. Rockeries, shade trees and peonies scattered naturally on a slope.

b. The garden's focal point—peony pavilion.

Figure 6-7 b

Figure 6-8 a

Figure 6-8 The Peony Garden in the western suburbs of Beijing.

a. A variety of peonies mixed with trees.

b. A statue of "peony goddess" viewed through a peony-shaped gateway at the garden entrance.

c. A fresco in the garden depicting legends connected with peony.

Figure 6-8 b

Figure 6-8 c

Figure 6-9 a

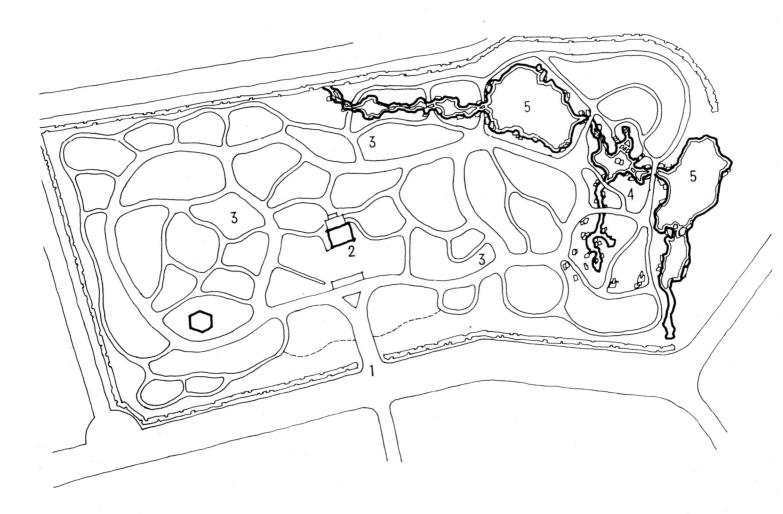

Figure 6-9 b

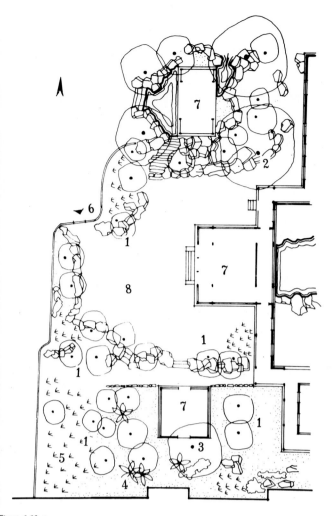

Figure 6-10 a

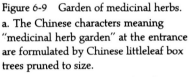

Figure 6-10 b

Figure 6-10 c

Figure 6-9   Garden of medicinal herbs.

a. The Chinese characters meaning "medicinal herb garden" at the entrance are formulated by Chinese littleleaf box trees pruned to size.

b. Plan: 1. Entrance. 2. "Studio of Medicinal Herbs" and the statue of Li Shizhen. 3. Cultivation area for medicinal herbs. 4. Area for moisture-tolerant herbs. 5. Water area.

Figure 6-10   A loquat garden.

a. Plan: 1. Loquat trees. 2. Schneider zelkova. 3. Chinese parasol trees. 4. Palms. 5. Bamboo groves. 6. Walls and entrance. 7. Building. 8. Brick-paved ground.

b. Sketch: The central compound in the loquat garden with loquat trees all around and visible from any one of these pavilions.

c. A corner of the loquat garden.

d. The garden entrance with loquat trees on both sides as markers.

Figure 6-10 d

IV. Plantings in "Inner Gardens"

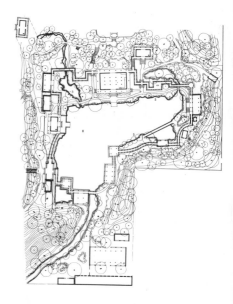

Figure 6-11 a

An "Inner Garden", or a garden within a garden, is usually separated from the rest of the garden space by walls, small hillocks, water or woods. It is a common feature in Chinese garden designs. Even in a natural scenic area or a large park, a small sector is sometimes set off as a separate garden different from the surrounding areas in style and content. It is relatively independent and more elegantly designed, and is often the main attraction.

The idea of building inner gardens is part of the traditional gardening art of China. Instead of unfolding before the beholder a panoramic view all at once, the designer prefers to lead him on from one interesting scene to another. A garden in a garden is created exactly to meet the requirements of the discriminating sightseer. The view varies from general to specific, from broad outline to details, leading the sightseers up to a point where they are likely to stop for closer observation and contemplation. Thus an inner garden often embodies the best of what Chinese gardens have to offer.

The Xie Qu Yuan (Garden of Harmony) inside the Summer Palace near Beijing is a typical inner garden in the ancient Chinese palace garden style. It covers an area of about 0.63 hectare, separated from the rest of the Summer Palace by hillocks, walls and trees. A pond makes up its main scene, forming a close space with the pond in the centre surrounded by buildings of different heights (figure 6-11). The plant disposition is characterized by large evergreen or deciduous trees grown on the hillocks and by the walls providing backgrounds for the buildings and creating the tranquil atmosphere necessary to an inner garden. Grown by the side of the water are mainly weeping willows occasionally mixed with a Chinese pine, a parasol tree or a Hankow willow to add variety to the canopy line. This is a traditional way of Chinese plant disposition, and presents a natural and graphic view of the surrounding buildings from under the plant canopies. When the branches of the willow trees swing in a gentle breeze, the fascination of movement is added.

Figure 6-11 b

Figure 6-11   The Xie Qu Yuan (Garden of Harmony) in Beijing's Summer Palace.

a. Plan: 1. Entrance. 2. Peach trees. 3. The Qing Qin Catchment, a water outlet. 4. Bamboo groves. 5. Weeping willows. 6. Lacebark pines. 7. Chinese pines. 8. Pond.

b. Scene I. The Fish-Study Bridge in the south and the canopy line in the west.

c. Scene II. The buildings in the east and the canopy line formed by various kinds of trees.

Figure 6-11 c

Figure 6-11 c

c. Sketches: Different canopy lines in
four directions. The canopy line of the
trees in the north is dwarfed by the large
main buildings. The buildings in the
other three directions are smaller; but
the canopy lines of the trees are
prominent, creating an overall balance.

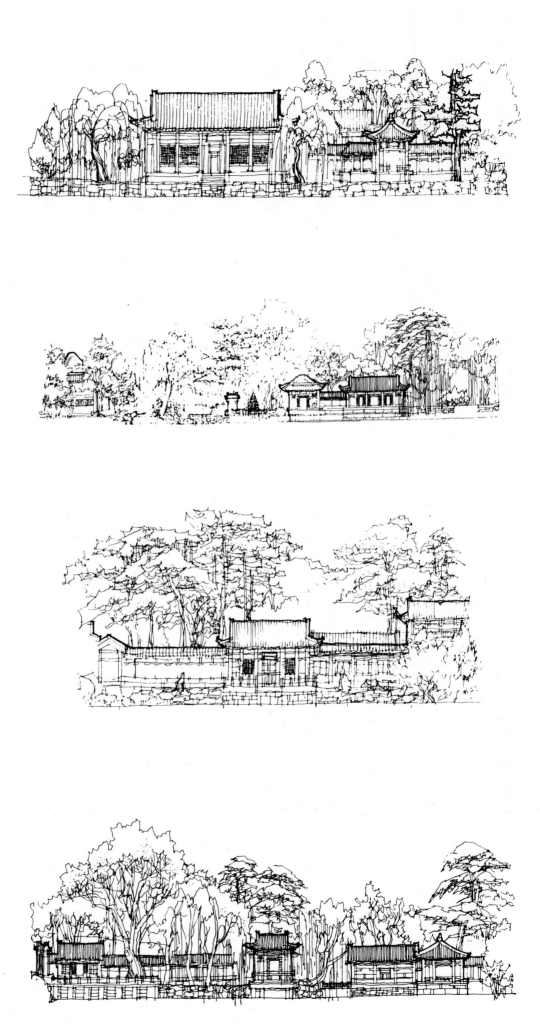

Figure 6-11 d

d. Scene III. The buildings and trees in
the northeast corner. The ornate round
pavilion and the walkways it connects
are matched by thin willow branches
and the green foliage around.

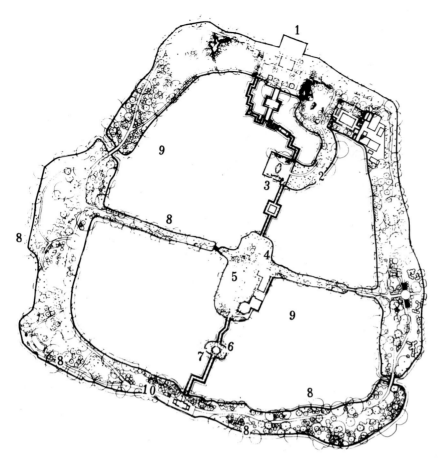

Figure 6-12 a

The colour pattern of the garden is rather simple. The basic colours are dark and light green. The waterlilies in the pond and some other flowers on the bank play only a colour accent role. This plant disposition is designed mainly to attract people to the picturesque buildings. However, at the northwest corner of the garden, there is a duct for water drainage designed to look like a streamlet in a gully. A small bridge is built over the murmuring water with rocks and earth piled up on both sides, forming steep banks. Grown on them are bamboo groves, silk tree, Chinese red bud, weeping forsythia, wistaria, peach tree and pear tree. Together they form an entity with dense flower and leaves distinctly different from its surroundings. While the Xie Qu Yuan is an inner garden of the Summer Palace, the streamlet and rockery form still another inner garden of the Xie Qu Yuan—a good illustration of the design, "a garden in a garden."

The Three Pools Mirroring the Moon in the West Lake in Hangzhou is another inner garden. It is a scenic spot by itself surrounded by the broad water surface of the West Lake, and divided into four water zones by cross-linked dikes (figure 6-12). The willow trees grown on the intersecting dikes plus the partitioned water surface enhance the perspective of the garden. Without this inner garden, this part of the lake would be a mere expanse of water.

The upper canopies of the plants on the dikes are composed of footcatkin willow, Hankow willow and weeping Hankow willow. These trees are grown freely at intervals of 4-10 m.

Although the three kinds of trees are all deciduous, they are in different shapes. The footcatkin willow has robust roots and are very resistant to water. The spreading sturdy

Figure 6-12 "Three Pools Mirroring the Moon" at the West Lake in Hangzhou.

a. Plan: 1. North dock. 2. Bamboo path. 3. Flowering peach trees. 4. Midway Pavilion. 5. Camphor trees. 6. Tablet pavilion. 7. Pygmy waterlilies. 8. Footcatkin willows. 9. Waterlilies. 10. Banana shrubs and other flowering plants.

b. A bird's-eye view of the "Three Pools Mirroring the Moon."

Figure 6-12 b

Figure 6-12 c

branches often tilt elegantly toward the water surface. The Hankow willow has long, slender branches swaying gracefully in the wind, and the Hankow weeping willow has round canopies with straight trunks and soft but dense branches. Alternate planting of the three kinds of willow trees on the long dikes presents a picture of both harmony and contrast. The choice of trees also suits seasonal changes. The leaves of footcatkin willow turn yellow by mid-November and last for a month, whereas the other two varieties turn yellow in early December and do not shed their leaves until the end of the year. During this period, the interplay of colours between the different trees offers an interesting sight. However, since they are all deciduous and wither in winter, some evergreen trees have been interplanted in recent years. In the meantime, flowers, particularly some low flowering shrubs and ground covers, are added on the banks where people frequently visit. For instance, in summer and autumn when people go to the south bank to enjoy the moon, fragrant flowers like banana shrub, osmanthus and common evening primrose are grown there to match the Chinese tradition of pairing full moon with beautiful flowers, or to infer to the Chinese legend that there is osmanthus on the moon. Other plantings on the banks include yulan magnolia, Japanese keria, common flowering quince and rose for spring, and camellia, plum and nandina for winter. Together, these plants enrich the scenery of all four seasons.

Since the water level fluctuates, some perennial flowers and shrubs are grown one metre from the water as cover crops. These plants include Italian reed, oxalis, dwarf lilyturf, roof iris and autumn zephyrlily. Sectors of the embankments are built of rockeries on which dwarf lilyturf and Chinese star jasmine grow in the crevices. The walls of the rest of the long embankments are overgrown with climbing fig to hide the bare man-made wall surface. The result is a natural green belt all along the embankments. As for the choice of aquatic plants, those with smaller flowers and leaves such as pygmy waterlilies are disposed for close enjoyment near the northern and southern causeways where there are many small elegant buildings and bridges. The waterlilies with large flowers and leaves are planted further away from the banks.

This island-shaped inner garden, the Three Pools Mirroring the Moon, covers an area of 70,000 m². At a distance, it almost looks like a boat on the 5.6-square-kilometre West Lake. Only after landing on the dike can people begin to relish the garden scenery with winding corridors, pavilions, curved paths and flourishing flowers and trees gradually unfolding before their eyes. This is indeed a unique inner garden hidden in a lake.

c. A panoramic view of the causeways planted mainly with footcatkin willows.

d. Plants on the causeways vary in height but methodically arranged to present a balanced view.

e. Climbing fig forms a green belt along the embankments to harmonize with the water colour and cover up the hard construction surface.

Figure 6-12 d

Figure 6-12 e

179

Afterword

I have been studying Chinese garden plantings for 30 years and have written articles about the subject. But this is my first book for foreign readers. I have tried to put into it some basic principles and a general introduction to the tradition and practice of plant disposition in Chinese gardens. My observations over the past 30 years have convinced me that the style of Chinese gardens today combines the traditions of ancient Chinese gardens with new customs and modern trends, plus some influences from outside China.

I owe much to the talent and work of Mr. Zheng Shuyang, Ms. Tian Qing, Mr. Wang Liyong and Mr. Ma Zenglin, who did the pictures. The book drew some material from my earlier book, a special research volume on plant disposition in Hangzhou gardens. Some of the material in the chapter on flower beds was provided by Ms. Zhu Xiuzhen.

Zhu Junzhen
Professor of Qinghua University

English Name	Botanical Name	English Name	Botanical Name
Ailanthus	Ailanthus	Chinese photinia	Photinia serrulata
Allspice pimenta	Pimenta dioica	Chinese pine	Pinus tabulaeformis
Alocasia	Alocasia	Chinese pink	Dianthus chinensis
Apricot	Prunus armeniaca	Chinese pistache	Pistacia chinensis
Augustine rhododendron	Rhododendron augustini	Chinese plum yew	Caphalotaxus fortunei
Autumn zephyrlily	Zephyranthes candida	Chinese redbud	Cercis chinensis
Azter dahlia	Dahlia pinnata	Chinese sapium	Sapium sebiferum
Aztec marigold	Tagetes erecta	Chinese scholar tree	Sophora japonica
Baldcypress	Taxodium	Chinese soapberry	Sapindus mukorossi
Balsa	Ochroma	Chinese star jasmine	Trachelospermum jasminoides
Balsam fir (Balsam)	Abies balsamea	Chinese St. Johnswort	Hypericum chinensis
Banana shrub	Michelia fuscata	Chinese trumpet creeper	Campsis grandiflora
Banks rose	Rosa banksiae	Chinese wingnut	Pterocarya stenoptera
Banyan	Ficus benghalensis	Citron	Citrus medica
Bayberry	Myrica	Common box	Buxus sempervirens
Bermuda grass	Cynodon dactylon	Common China aster	Callistephus chinensis
Bigfruit elm	Ulmus macrocarpa	Common cockscomb	Celosia cristata
Bigleaf hydrangea	Hydrangea macrophylla	Common evening primrose	Oenothera biennis
Black bamboo	Phyllostachys nigra	Common flowering quince	Chaenomeles lagenaria
Black locust	Robinia pseudoacacia	Common four-o'clock	Mirabilis jalapa
Black poplar	Populus nigra	Common poinsettia	Euphorbia pulcherrima
Bo tree	Ficus religiosa	Common snapdragon	Antirrhinum majus
Bracket plant	Chlorophytum capense	Common tulip	Tulipa gesneriana
Broadleaf sasa	Sasa fessellata	Copper alternanthera	Alternanthera versicolor
Broom cypress	Kochia scoparia	Cork oak	Quercus suber
Buckeye	Aesculus	Cottonrose hibiscus	Hibiscus mutabilis
Buffalo grass	Buchloe dactyloides	Cottonwood	Populus deltoides
Buttonwood	Platanus orientalis	Crapemyrtle	Lagerstroemia
Camellia	Camellia	Creeping dayflower	Commelina nudiflora
Camphor tree	Cinnamomum camphora	Creeping fig tree	Ficus pumila
Cape jasmine	Gardenia jasminoides	Creeping oxalis	Oxalis corniculata
Catalpa	Catalpa	Cut-leaved maple	Acer dissectum
China cotton	Gossypium arboreum var. nanking	Daimyo oak	Quercus dentata
		Daisy	Bellis
Chinese aucuba	Aucuba chinensis	Daylily	Hemerocallis
Chinese chestnut	Castanea bungeana	Deodar cedar	Cedrus deodara
Chinese flowering crabapple	Malus spectabilis	Dogwood	Cornus
Chinese hackberry	Celtis senensis	Dragon cypress	Sabina chinensis var. kaizuca
Chinese hawthorn	Crataegus pinnatifida	Dragon spruce	Picea asperata
Chinese juniper	Juniperus chinensis	Dwarf clubmosses	Selaginellaceae
Chinese littleleaf box	Buxus microphylla var. sinica	Dwarf lilyturf	Ophiopogon japonicus
Chinese mahonia	Mahonia fortunei	Ebony	Diospyros
Chinese parasol tree	Firmiana simplex	Edible canna	Canna edulis
Chinese peony	Paeonia albiflora	Eucommia	Eucommia ulmoides

English Name	Botanical Name	English Name	Botanical Name
Evergreen chinkapin	*Castanopsis*	Panicled goldrain tree	*Koelreuteria paniculata*
Faber maple	*Acer fabri*	Plantain banana	*Musa paradisiaca*
Feverfew chrysanthemum	*Chrysanthemum parthenium*	Potmarigold calendula	*Calendula officinalis*
Florists chrysanthemum	*Chrysanthemum morifolium*	Purpleleaf plum	*Prunus cerasifera var. atropurpurea*
Footcatkin willow	*Salix magnifica*		
Fortune fontanesia	*Fontanesia fortunei*	Pygmy waterlily	*Nymphaea tetragona*
Fortunes windmill palm	*Trachycarpus fortunei*	Roof iris	*Iris tectorum*
Garden balsam	*Impatiens balsamina*	Saucer magnolia	*Magnolia soulangeana*
Garden pansy	*Viola tricolor var. hortensis*	Sawtooth oak	*Quercus acutissima*
Glossy privet	*Ligustrum lucidum*	Scarlet kafirlily	*Clivia miniata*
Hankow willow	*Salix matsudana*	Scarlet sage	*Salvia splendens*
Henon bamboo	*Phyllostachys nigra var. henonsis*	Schneider zelkova	*Zelkova schneideriana*
India canna	*Canna indica*	Seal flower	*Dicentra spectabilis*
Indian azalea	*Rhododendron simsii*	Seven-sisters	
Ivy	*Hedera*	Siberian elm	*Ulmus pumila*
Japanese black pine	*Pinus thunbergii*	Silkoak grevillea	*Grevillea robusta*
Japanese cinnamon	*Cinnamomum pedunculatum*	Silk tree	*Albizzia julibrissin*
Japanese creeper	*Parthenocissus tricuspidata*	Slenderer lady palm	*Rhapis humilis*
Japanese kerria	*Kerria japonica*	Smoke tree	*Cotinus*
Japanese lawngrass	*Zoysia japonica*	Snow azalea	*Rhododendron mucronatum*
Japanese maple	*Acer palmatum*	Southern magnolia	*Magnolia grandiflora*
Japanese pagoda tree	*Sophora japonica*	Sweet osmanthus	*Osmanthus fragrans*
Japanese rose	*Rosa multiflora var. platyphylla*	Sweet viburnum	*Viburnum odoratissimum*
Japanese white pine	*Pinus parviflora*	Tallow tree	*Sapium sebiferum*
Java bishopwood	*Bischofia javanica*	Tatarian aster	*Aster tataricus*
Jujube	*Zizyphus*	Thunberg spiraea	*Spiraea thunbergi*
Korean ash	*Fraxinus rhynchophylla*	Tobira pittosporum	*Pittosporum tobira*
Korean velvet grass	*Zoysia tenuifolia*	Tonkin cane	*Arundinaria amabilis*
Larch	*Larix*	Torch lily	*Kniphofia*
Lilac	*Syringa*	Trident maple	*Acer buergerianum*
Lilac daphne	*Daphne genkwa*	Truncate-leaved maple	*Acer truncatum*
Loquat	*Eriobotrya japonica*	Tuftwool rhododendron	*Rhododendron floccigerum*
Lovely golden larch	*Pseudolarix amabilis*	Ural falsespiraea	*Sorbaria sorbifloria*
Lusterleaf holly	*Ilex latifolia*	Varnish tree	*Rhus verniciflua*
Manchu rose	*Rose xanthina*	Weeping forsythia	*Forsythia suspensa*
Masson pine	*Pinus massoniana*	Weeping Hankow willow	*Salix matsudana var. suspensa*
Metasequoia	*Metasequoia glyptostroboides*	White common lilac	*Syringa vulgaris var. alba*
Myrobalan plum	*Prunus cerasifera*	Winter jasmine	*Jasminum nudiflorum*
Nandina	*Nandina domestica*	Wintersweet	*Chimonanthus praecox*
Oleander	*Nerium*	Wistaria	*Wistaria*
Oriental plane tree	*Platanus orientalis*	Yew podocarpus	*Podocarpus macrophylla*
Oriental sweetgum	*Liquidambar orientalis*	Yulan magnolia	*Magnolia denudata*

中国园林植物配置艺术

朱钧珍　著

*

外文出版社出版

（中国北京百万庄路 24 号）

邮政编码 100037

精美彩色印刷有限公司印刷

1992 年（8 开）第一版

（英）

ISBN 7—119—01252—5/J·852（外）

15000（精）